TREE-HOUSES

AND OTHER MODERN HIDEAWAYS

ANDREAS WENNING

DOM
publishers

INDEX

PREFACE

'*Of Other Spaces* is an essay title by Michel Foucault, which has influenced the discourse on space in recent decades. He says analogously that (real) places are outside of all places, even though it may be possible to indicate their location in reality. The philosopher calls them 'heterotopias' because, in contrast to utopias, they are concrete places which also represent counterpoles or buttresses in everyday space. Gardens are such places, as are cinemas, museums, libraries or funfairs ... a treehouse too may be classified as a heterotopia. As concrete as its location in a real, existing tree may be, the house reaching high up into the crown of the tree, is literally 'removed'. It is a house without foundations, yet still completely rooted. A childhood dream – of both freedom and security – is made real.'

Going back about sixteen years, I used the foregoing sentences in an architecture discussion for the *Taz* newspaper to introduce a description of an unusual project by a younger architect from Bremen. But what does 'unusual' mean? When Andreas Wenning invited me to visit his treehouse, I was initially sceptical. I associated the term 'treehouse' with a whole range of clichés. It made me think of DIY dads, and I knew that there were many bizarre examples of treehouses, particularly in England. Sure, I thought, the treehouse is a marginal note in architecture – but is it really a subject to be taken seriously? One sunny day in early autumn, we travelled by train to Bassum. From there, after cycling through the countryside for around half an hour, we reached Groß Henstedt – scattered farmhouses in a landscape of gently rolling hills. One of these farmhouses belonged to an acquaintance of Wenning, and this was where the architect had built his treehouse in a clump of beeches, right behind the chicken-run. There it was, swaying among the trees, ten metres above our heads by guess. Its shape appeared unusual. It was based on the shape of an equilateral triangle coming to a point, thus awakening associations with the bow of a ship or rather, perhaps, an UFO. In any event, my first clichéd expectation of a romantic ancient hut, high up in the treetops, was not fulfilled – which immediately pleased me. The high-tech associations were, however, only partially right. Despite the technically business-like craftsmanship, the material used – this being larch – actually lends the treehouse a more rustic look. The same applies to its steep ladder, by means of which we now climbed up to the treehouse. Arriving at the top, we entered a narrow cabin with a platform covered in wool felt – a place for relaxing. A skylight affords a view of the dense branches beneath the green beech roof and then a farther glimpse into the blue, grey or star-studded sky. From a freestanding seat on the obtuse side of the triangle, one's glance falls on a paddock.

I had met Andreas Wenning a few years earlier. He was one of the leading activists of the younger generation of architects in Bremen who met at the *Young Architects' Forum*. Having completed their studies, most of his fellow members found themselves in precarious and unsatisfying jobs. They battled against dejection by undertaking common campaigns, organising workshops and events called *Lost Places* or *Night Storage*. So now Wenning had built himself a treehouse in the country. Was this a withdrawal from his earlier activities? A retreat into seclusion? The situation was, in fact, quite different. Andreas Wenning explained to me that this treehouse was merely a prototype. His plan was to offer the planning and construction of treehouses to the public at large under the name of *Baumraum* (tree space). As such, the treehouse which we had viewed together was a kind of experimental structure, to explore the potential for other, more sophisticated and larger treehouses with bigger budgets. So it was an architectural business idea for filling a niche in the tight market of planning services. I must admit that I was sceptical – something which I didn't want to display so clearly to my architect acquaintance. He however seemed so convinced of his idea that it was unlikely my doubts had much impact on him. After this meeting, I lost touch with Andreas Wenning. We would run into each other now and again at the railway station when he was heading off to or returning from a business appointment. He indicated that *Baumraum* was quite successful. I was therefore all the more surprised when I recently discovered from a work report the dimensions that the project had meanwhile taken on. One can meanwhile marvel at a good five dozen treehouses in a huge variety of styles, scattered around the globe. To some extent, the treehouses are perhaps somewhat smoother, certainly more professionally finished, than his first treehouse

which we looked at together back then. Even at that time, Wenning advocated a modern treehouse over a nostalgic look and post-modern playfulness. He has long since refined the not quite resolved contradiction between futuristic design and handmade look apparent in his first test treehouse, by offering two alternatives. Expressed somewhat simplistically, one could describe the two types as 'capsule' and 'hut', chosen depending on whether one desires a contrast or wishes the treehouse to blend in with the natural surroundings. If one examines Andreas Wenning's design studies, one might suspect that he personally prefers the first type. The many layers of production make it clear that the given local situation, together with budget, and the builder's needs and aesthetic preferences, can lead to highly personalised solutions: on the one hand, there are sturdy constructions with simple finishings, on the other, futuristically designed and luxurious variants. The techniques with which the treehouses are connected with the trees are also significant: depending on static requirements various innovative and tree-friendly solutions are used. At times the treehouses hang in the branches of the trees without supports or stand on several, slender supports which are reminiscent of pick-up sticks.

Why do people today want treehouses? The sociologist Gerhard Schulze coined the phrase 'thrill-seeking society' to describe a certain drive which is currently prevalent. The desire to experience something special exists across almost all social milieus, while the variety

of individual products and 'how to' manuals on the 'market for experiences' (Schulze: 'Erlebnismarkt'), has achieved an overwhelming profusion, precisely in order to offer this 'something special'. The treehouse is just such a special experience. It offers a primordial spatial and sensual experience, close to nature, while demonstrating the uniqueness, the individuality of its owner. In terms of experience options, a treehouse is certainly not one of the worst, whereby its above-mentioned heterotopian character also plays a role. Its remoteness turns this space amongst the trees into a place for dreaming and contemplation.

EBERHARD SYRING

TREEHOUSES

Treehouses have a long tradition in human history. Some of our ancestors were already building tree dwellings many thousands of years ago. Their height and concealment amongst branches and leaves offered protection against dangerous animals and enemies. As such, life in and with the trees was of existential importance. For many species of animal and for some primitive peoples this is still the case today. Later, man discovered the tree's recreational uses. The house in the treetop developed from a place which was essential to survival into what might be described as a luxury commodity, and became a synonym for adventure, romance and freedom. It became a playground and an attractive challenge for children and adults alike. In art, literature, and film, the treehouse has been the backdrop for many scenarios ranging from the magical to the futuristic. Opinions differ with regard to the questions of what defines a treehouse, or at what point a structure deserves that name. For some, the treehouse must be fully anchored in the tree and may not be connected to the ground with any kind of support. I do not entirely agree with this strict definition. In my opinion, treehouses are buildings or structures which stand in a close dialogue with trees in spatial or design terms. A treehouse never stands directly on the ground. It is removed from the earth's surface and is very close to the tree. It may encompass part of the tree, or its structure may respond to the tree's growth. In this sense, the sensual wish to get closer to the trees, to enjoy the view and experience nature in a special way are the determining motivations. If the tree is too small or too weak to hold the treehouse, supports can be employed without the resulting structure having to forgo the title of 'treehouse'. The interplay between built structure and natural life form should be harmonious. what is crucial is that the tree is not overweighted, that it has the necessary space to move in the wind and that it can continue growing without obstruction. The highest requirement is that the treehouse fits in with its natural surroundings and not vice versa. The style of the construction depends on the builder's taste. Generally speaking, treehouses tend to be associated with a fairy tale, traditional vernacular. They are often little huts in the tree with gabled roof or lattice windows. This comes close to the classic image of the ancient hut and can certainly have charm. Astonishingly, the fact that treehouses can also be designed in contemporary style and with modern furnishings almost amounts to a new discovery. Such buildings are opening up a new area in architecture which few planners have considered as part of their remit to date. The 'treehouse' is increasingly being discovered by students as a design playground, and is rarely constructed by planners in modern form. This may be due to the generally small level of planning required and the correspondingly lower fee prospects, or it may be because of the special nature of planning around a living 'foundation'. In many respects, designing and building a treehouse can be compared with any other constructional work, and presents similar challenges to the planner. The unique nature and beauty of such a task lies in engaging with the trees. The designer also has to deal with the perception of the natural space and the very personal wishes of the client. It is a question of creating a space in which one enjoys a particular sense of well-being, where one may enjoy cosiness, adventure, a special kind of privacy and, above all, proximity to nature. These spaces may be in trees, but they can also be on the water, in the desert, in the ice, or on the roof of a city high-rise.

ANDREAS WENNING

A BRIEF DIGRESSION ON LIVING IN TREES

THROUGHOUT THE AGES, TREEHOUSES HAVE BEEN BUILT AS PLACES OF PLEASURE AND HOSPITALITY. THE FOLLOWING CHAPTER PROVIDES A BRIEF OVERVIEW WITH A FEW SELECTED EXAMPLES.

A LOOK BACK THROUGH HISTORY

We know that materials which were already alive in the early classical period were used to construct housing. In ancient Egypt bowers were covered with climbing plants to provide shade in the hot, dry desert climate. Sources indicate that in ancient Roman times too, treehouses were built for pleasure and to lighten up the appearance of villa gardens. Pliny the Elder's *Natural History* written in 77 A.D. mentions two treehouses, built in stately plane trees. The Roman emperor Caligula had one of them at his estate in Velitrae. This notorious emperor is said to have described his treehouse as a 'nest' and invited guests to banquet there. As reported by the description, the treehouse had enough space for 15 guests as well as the requisite servants. According to Pliny, the second treehouse in Lycia was in a hollow tree trunk. Its owner, Licinius Mucianus, the Consul of the region, was also accustomed to dine with his retinue in the tree. It is said that Licinius felt better there than in his magnificent marble mansions. The descriptions provided in the texts by Pliny, one of the most important authors of ancient times, influenced the writers of the Renaissance in Italy, who shared this fascination for lofty structures. It is possible that the details of treehouses which appeared in Francesco Colonna's novel *Hypnerotomachia Poliphili*, published in 1499, may also have influenced the nobility and rich of Italy. The Medici family had treehouses built in their gardens. These structures were widely admired and employed as a motif in literature and art. Moving from Italy to England, one should note what is believed to be the oldest surviving treehouse in the world. The treehouse at Pitchford Hall near Shrewsbury was first mentioned in 1714 and has been converted and renovated several times since then. It has a square floor plan and is integrated into an ancient lime tree. After its first golden age in the 16th and 17th centuries, the treehouse declined in popularity, but cultivated life amongst the trees enjoyed a comeback during the Romantic period when there was a greater appreciation of unspoilt nature.

Treehouse restaurant in Parc Robinson near Paris, France

Parc Robinson near Paris was the setting of an impressive treehouse project in the 19th century. The restaurateur Joseph Gueusquin was enthralled by a gigantic chestnut tree and built a restaurant, *Au Grand Robinson*, in it. A second treehouse restaurant, known as *Le Vrai Arbre de Robinson*, was built shortly afterwards directly opposite.

DANCING UNDER THE VILLAGE LIME TREE

In Germany, trees – especially lime trees – have been used as a place for festivals and dancing for centuries. Dancing under the lime trees dates back to the Middle Ages. Martin Luther mentioned lime trees being used for dancing and pleasure. In order to provide a worthy setting for a feast, large wooden scaffolding was erected beneath the lowest branches of the tree which, according to mythology, were intended for mankind's use. In addition to dancers, there was space for an entire group of musicians. The construction, which was sometimes on several levels, was built on up to twelve stone pillars. Steps would be cut into some of the lime trees, so that dance floors were actually created within the tree's branches.

In Peesten, Bavaria, there is a charming example with an upper storey which has an area of almost 90 square metres. People can dance beneath, on and in the tree. The branches of the lime trees would be manipulated and cut while they were still young, so that the forks of the branches would grow out evenly all round at a height of approximately 2.5 metres. In Bavaria, the 'Kunigunde Lime' in Kasberg has such a great circumference that six couples could dance on it at the same time. These lime trees were situated in places which had their own jurisdictions. In larger parishes, they mostly fell victim to new buildings. The practice of dancing and feasting beneath the lime trees very closely resembles the nature of a treehouse and shares the same roots. The beauty of the trees, as well as their powerful and romantic aura, are an invitation to linger and revel. Even today, one can still view – and perhaps even dance in – some of Germany's few intact 'dance limes', for example in Effelder, Peesten, and Sachsenbrunn.

Village lime tree in Peesten, Germany

Kittymag Treehouse, TreeHouse Company, UK

TREEHOUSES IN THE ENGLISH LANDSCAPED GARDEN

It is a striking phenomenon that a great number of treehouses have been and still are being built in England. This love of treehouses seems to lie in the British garden culture which, in contrast to the rigid and formal French Baroque and garden architecture, permitted more freedom of design. In the 18th century, when the country was becoming a world power, England's enlightened, liberal society was longing for paradise lost. This yearning for more poetry became apparent in landscape gardening when the garden was separated from the architecture to become an independently composed green space. English gardens and parks were more reminiscent of nature and were designed with various, constantly repeated style features. Important elements included waterways and lakes, natural paths, hills and a low wall which enclosed the whole. The entire garden, which is enhanced with sculptures and little buildings, was arranged like a painting. The decorative buildings in the garden could be reproductions of ruined castles and little chapels, Roman ruins, Turkish mosques or Chinese pagodas. Pavilions and treehouses were also built at a later period in time. These were used as meeting points, where tea might occasionally be served. This love of nature, of shaping green spaces and small buildings in gardens – has remained intact in England. This tradition may well explain why it is that in the UK several hundred treehouses, both large and small, have been built in recent decades – either by the owners themselves or by professionals.

Puget Sound in Gig Harbor, TreeHouse Workshop, USA

TREEHOUSES AS AN ALTERNATIVE LIVING SPACE

Our built environment is largely character-ised by traditions, standards and laws. Natu-rally, these laws are often very useful and have proven their value in many cases. However, peo-ple are constantly looking for ways to both liber-ate themselves from this restrictive framework, and to freely shape the space in which they live. Living among nature can play a major role here. There is barely any other country which has a greater tradition of free and experimental build-ing – and building close to nature – than North America. This is owing to the USA's origins as a country of immigration, where people often had to create homes in unconventional ways. The size of the country and vast expanses of open space offered the best opportunities for experimental building in natural surroundings. The term 'self-made architecture' describes a self-determined way of planning which is typical of the USA and may often be found there. Examples of it include houses made with recycled building materials, and unusual or artistically designed houses, both on the ground and in the trees. The treehouses built in Canada or the USA are frequently differ-ent to their European relatives in terms of size and liveability. Some have several floors and can be lived in all year round. The fact that even the treehouses are larger and higher in America is due to the previously mentioned wealth of free space, as well as building legislation which is occasionally laxer and the many fantastic trees. These are all qualities which a treehouse builder in Central Europe might well envy.

PROTESTS IN THE TREES

Left and right: West runway, eviction of Hüttendorf, Germany

In modern times, treehouses have been associated not only with romance, adventure, and play, or survival. They have also become places of protest. The destruction of natural habitats and our environment in all parts of the world for many decades and right into the present time must be one of the worst aspects of our civilisation. Because of economic interests, lack of knowledge and wilful ignorance the foundations of life on earth have been and still are being constantly altered and destroyed. Awareness of the value of nature and the urgent need to protect it have increased in recent decades. The birth and growth of environmental awareness worldwide is largely due to the dedication of environmentalists and activists. In particular, forests and individual trees in diverse locations throughout the world have often been the setting for demonstrations. In the activists' struggle to save forests and trees, treehouses have also played a significant role, and it is worth mentioning a few of them here.

West runway, one of the treehouses of Hüttendorf, Germany

West runway, eviction of Hüttendorf, Germany

WEST RUNWAY

At the beginning of the 1980s, plans were afoot to build an additional runway at Frankfurt airport, requiring the clearance of several hectares of forest. A citizens' action group was formed to campaign against the airport's expansion and the felling of the trees. After various fruitless attempts, activists and environmentalists built a hut where information on the airport expansion plans and their consequences was provided. When some demonstrators started staying there overnight in summer 1980, more and more structures were built until, finally, a village with over 70 huts had been created. At the same time, this action served as a peaceful protest against the clearance. As part of the tree protest, the *Young Socialists'* treehouse was also built in the area of the proposed runway. Because it was more difficult for the eviction forces to gain access to the treehouse, it became an important bastion of the resistance movement. In October of that year, the forest area outside of Hüttendorf was cleared. During this period, confrontation between demonstrators and police reached its peak, occasionally resulting in bloody violence. The peaceful protest action was transformed into a state resembling civil war. In November 1981 hundreds of policemen moved in to forcibly remove the protesters, and the Hüttendorf and treehouse were then razed to the ground. The protest failed to achieve its goal. Nor could a petition with 220.000 signatures prevent the forest clearance. The runway was officially inaugurated on the 12th of April 1984.

HAMBACH
FOREST

Treehouses have also recently become very important in the movement against deforestation in connection with what I see as misguided energy or transport policies. I expressly support the activists and admire their commitment, courage and creativity.

A particular environment for this dispute, in which treehouses played a central role, was and is Hambach Forest. Over the years, a large number of treehouses have been built there, which impress and touch me in many ways.

At this point I would like to give an activist and co-builder of treehouses in Hambach Forest a space for his thoughts and his impressions. As much as I'd like to introduce him by name, due to the politics involved, he prefers to remain anonymous. Still, I would like to thank him very much for his commitment and his contribution.

ANDREAS WENNING

A TREEHOUSE VILLAGE IN HAMBACH FOREST, 2017

A TREEHOUSE IN COMPANY

'Bolo! Bolo!' The shouts wake me up. I am lying in a small house in a huge oak tree. Pale autumn light filters through the large windows. Bolo, that's the name of this treehouse. Searchingly I look out the window, through the autumn colored crowns, to the neighboring tree. There, on the balcony of a larger treehouse, a friend stands and points to the forest floor twenty metres below us. Motionless, as if someone had turned them off and forgotten them, stand five policemen in combat uniforms with shields, helmets and protectors. A dog tugs at the chain one of them is holding. They are standing in a circle around the tree in whose crown I just woke up. Also with my friend are five other black-clad policemen, seemingly unconcerned, standing around the tree. Halfway up, one of the climbing ropes hangs in the light wind.

I lie back in bed and turn on my radio and cell phone one after the other and put coffee water on the gas stove. I don't think I'll be able to get down today. Today they are clearing.

I hear a huge crash, very close to me. Just a few hundred metres from me, large trees, similar to the one I am on, are being cut down. That's why the police are standing almost motionless under the busy trees. To arrest us in case we try to come down to prevent the clearing work.

Two scouts near the clearing operations report in. 'Someone managed to get up into one of the trees they're going to cut!' it crackles through the radio. From the other treehouses and through the radio, I hear cheers. It's so simple, I think. We're sitting in the tree and it can't be cut down. And if the tree doesn't fall, then lignite can't continue to be mined. Then the lignite can't be burned

either. As a result, fewer pollutants are released into our air. The man-made climate crisis could be slowed down a bit and so there might be a chance to save our future.

Since 2012, the Hambach Forest has been inhabited by people. Most of the forest and several villages that are also inhabited have already disappeared in the Hambach open pit mine in the Rhenish lignite mining area. The lignite mining area is the largest source of CO_2 in Europe. The solution seems simple: come here and stop the destruction.

A fight of David against Goliath, of the inhabitants of the beautiful treehouses on one side and the evil, overpowering corporation and the brutal police on the other side?

The more I think about it, read and research how it could come to this, the more I realise that the

situation here is much more complicated and far-reaching. The policeman under my tree is not standing there because he wants to. Maybe he likes what he's doing, maybe he doesn't, but it doesn't matter. He has to sell a large part of his life, and sometimes his conscience, in order to have access to what he needs to live. It is the same with the miners in the opencast mine, the employees of RWE and myself. No one has the malicious goal of destroying the lives of people here or indirectly in other parts of the world.

But it happens anyway. And all of them are part of it with their actions, because it is suggested to them. I can understand them.

But what kind of society is it that encourages people to act in such a destructive and senseless way against their own needs, against their future?

My head is pounding. The longer I lie in the treehouse listening to the falling of the trees, the more my insides clench. I stare at the boards of Bolo's inner lining. These boards used to be spruce trees in the gigantic forestry complexes of Russia. There they were felled, sawed and nailed together into pallets. Again, by people who do this because they need the money to live. As a base for goods of all kinds, the pallet has traveled the world and, loaded with energy-intensively produced goods, has been transported to the place where it can be sold most

profitably. And this by people who also do this only because otherwise they could not buy anything from these very goods. Until the spruce wood could not be used any further and the pallets were to be disposed of. We dragged them into the forest, took them apart with crowbars and used the boards to build treehouses.

Why can't we as a society just do what makes such obvious sense: stop the climate crisis, distribute resources so that no one goes hungry, end wars, and try to get the best possible life for everyone one on this planet out of it?

And as I ponder this, I realise what the treehouses actually stand for here and why they fascinate so many people. They stand not only for our will to resist deforestation. Or for the risk that we are willing to take so high above the ground, with policemen below us. They stand for a different way of living in society.

Everything about this treehouse bears traces of this. All the knots and climbing equipment, the roof construction and the suspension bridge to the next tree are not here because it is profitable, but because it makes sense. Thousands of people have been here and participated in its creation: They have shared piece by piece what they knew and owned, without patents, contracts and cost-benefit maximisation. The pallet boards from the

wall someone has leveraged in painstaking work, but with enthusiasm, from the pallet that another had previously carried hundreds of metres into the forest. So many hands were involved in building this house, cooking for everyone during construction, transporting the material into the forest, that it seems absurd to claim the house here is my property.

Every morning we come together over suspension bridges and across ropes on the largest treehouse and discuss what needs to be done, what makes sense. We discuss who needs what and who can help where. Who will cook for everyone and who will communicate with the press. I think about the knot where the treehouse hangs in the tree. Even right now, my life literally hangs on the work of other people. Of people, some of whom I have never seen or met. This treehouse is proof that another society is possible. As a tiny touch of utopia, it hides from the motionless policemen in the crowns that are inaccessible to them. And every person who has ever set out to climb into the crown of a tree with a little effort and risk knows that a new world opens up there that could hardly be imagined from below.

And even if the noise of the chain saws takes my breath away, I know: even if all the treehouses are destroyed, this world remains.

EPILOGUE

In 2017, after two days of clearing, amid massive and diverse protests, tree occupations, and nationwide actions, a court decided to halt clearing for the season. For the first time in forty years, a clearing season (October to March) had been prevented.

Police operations and partial evacuations in Hambach Forest continued. Nevertheless, countless people joined the protest locally and around the world in 2018. Over fifty treehouses were erected during this period. In September 2018, the government of North Rhine-Westphalia decided to launch the largest police operation in the history of North Rhine-Westphalia and began the evacuation of the entire forest. Under massive violence, the life-threatening operation was not ended even when a friend of ours fell and died. After more than a month, almost the entire forest was without treehouses. The way was clear for the coming logging season.

A large demonstration, to which several tens of thousands of people were expected, was about to take place when the Higher Administrative Court once again decreed that the forest was not to be cleared in the coming years. The demonstration became a celebration of joy. Two months later, there were more treehouses in the forest than ever before. In the lignite phase-out law, the federal government stipulated that Hambach Forest would not be cleared. To the right and left, the excavators are to continue eating away, wiping out villages, turning the forest into an island. In other places in the Rhenish coalfield, too, coal will continue to be mined and used to generate electricity until 2038. CO_2 emissions will continue to be emitted to such an extent that it is hardly possible to speak of a fair contribution to combating climate change and keeping within the 1.5 degree limit.

The symptoms of the climate crisis are increasing noticeably and measurably. More and more people and other living beings are losing their livelihoods in the everyday madness of growth, profit maximisation and wage dependency.

So it is more urgent than ever to get moving and create what these treehouses have shown me: a better society. It is possible, and it is time to reach for it and risk something for it.

THE TREE PEOPLE

THE KOROWAI OF IRIAN JAYA, INDONESIA

The Korowai live in the Irian Jaya region, the most westerly part of New Guinea, which belongs to Indonesia. They are one of the last few primitive peoples who still retain Stone Age lifestyles. Experts estimate that around 1.500 to 3.000 members of this people still live in Papua. Their culture is not familiar with iron or other metals; they have no writing and have not developed any pottery. To the north of the Dairam Kabur river, their habitat extends to the mountains. To the southwest it reaches from the Senggo mission station to the Eilanden river. They are hunter-gatherers, living off frogs, insects, and snakes.

They hunt the few available animals with bow and arrow. Their staple food is sago, a nutritious starch which they obtain from the sago palm. Their tools are stone axes, bone knives, the sago hammer, and sticks for digging. The few newer tools that they possess, such as machetes or metal knives, were given to them by missionaries or other visitors. The really special feature of the Korowai culture, however, is how they live: in the upper levels of the rainforest. This is an almost completely obsolete tradition, which was still practised a few centuries ago by primitive peoples in many areas of the South

Seas, along the equator. Their treehouses are usually 5 to 17 metres above the ground and have a floor area of around 30 square metres. Some are even built in breathtaking heights of up to 50 metres above the forest floor.
The Korowai select ancestral places to build their treehouses, where they then create clearings in the dense jungle. The host trees are often high wambon or banyan trees, in which they integrate their lightweight constructions. To build the houses, the crowns of the trees are sometimes lopped off, so that only the trunk is used as a supporting column. For higher treehouses the

Korowai also build directly in the crowns of both living and dead trees. Because of the surplus of vegetation, the Korowai do not need to be sparing with the trees. To build the treehouses, they use straight branches for the basic frame and opened--out pieces of bark for flooring. The leaves of the sago palm are used for the roof and as a wall covering. The treehouses have a limited life span of around two to five years. Once the structures are damaged or no longer usable, new treehouses are simply built elsewhere. Men and women live together in the same treehouse but in separate quarters. Each gender has its own half, which the other is not permitted to enter. The Korowai children live with their mothers. Fire is highly valued by this people. As such, each treehouse has a fireplace which is used to prepare food and also marks the centre of the sleeping quarters. The fire is made in a wooden basket with clay and leaves. It is suspended from rattan fibres into a hole in the floor of the treehouse. If the fire threatens to get out of hand, the rattan cords are simply cut and the fire basket falls to the ground. The Korowai live in treehouses for a wide variety of spiritual and practical reasons. Life in the trees offers them protection from wild animals, tropical diseases, and flooding. Living at a height also has an important protective function in terms of hostilities between the family clans, of which there are approximately 250. According to the beliefs of this primitive people, the treehouse also protects against black magic. The Indonesian government considers these people to be godless creatures, unworthy of protection. When it comes to exploiting mineral resources and clearing the forests, they are an obstacle. Sadly, it is only a matter of time before the Korowai's way of life vanishes altogether, forever destroying one of the last primitive peoples.

Treehouses at a height of 40 metres, Gibbon Experience, Bokeo, North Laos

PUBLIC TREEHOUSES

Some years ago the tourism industry also discovered the uses of treehouses. The trend towards more ecology and the greater need for nature have increased demand for this kind of exotic accommodation. The spectrum ranges from simple tree shelters to luxuriously equipped treehouses, which can now be booked in many parts of the world. Furnishings depend on climatic conditions and on whether or not the rooms can be furnished with electricity and water, and are connected to a sewerage system. Many providers use the very media-friendly term 'treehouse hotel to woo customers. On closer inspection, not all such accommodations have earned this title. Thus a 'treehouse' often actually proves to be a cottage on the ground, which, by coincidence rather than design, happens to stand close to a tree. In Asia, there are some accommodations in the trees which are indirectly used to protect the rainforest. By practising sensitive, green tourism, the value of the forest is made tangible and jobs are created for locals. The revenue is used to pay gamekeepers or to purchase further areas of rainforest and, if possible, to have them protected. The construction style of tree hotels varies widely and is usually based on the given country's old, traditional style or reproduces the buildings of times long past. Not all public treehouses are used as hotels. Some rooms in the trees house restaurants or, in leisure parks, may be viewed or explored. The scope for developing and implementing exciting projects in and around trees is huge.

Children's treehouse in Frankfurt/Main, Germany

THE LITTLE ARCHITECTS

In many parts of the world – and particularly in Europe – there is a longstanding tradition of children building treehouses. Either they do this by themselves or they are given advice and practical help by their mothers, fathers, or grandparents. The reason for such activity seems to be obvious: It is fun and promises adventure – not only for the children. The little house in the trees often entails a 'childhood dream'. Fondly regarded and a repository of fantasies, it is a place which appears to be removed from everyday space. Children have long been fans of the treehouse since it provides them with many things they cannot find elsewhere: It is a space which they create and use themselves. In most cases, treehouses are built without great planning. The choice of materials used is often determined by what is on hand: a few old planks, a bit of metal sheeting, a couple of nails, and a gnarled cherry tree are enough to get things moving. The tree's state of health or deeper considerations such as statics are seldom taken into account when building starts. The spontaneity involved in designing a treehouse often leads to wonderful results and qualities which buildings created by adult 'experts' can only dream of. In building and living in a treehouse creativity, craftsmanship, climbing skills and perhaps courage are all required. The treehouse can be a collective task for both children and adults. It is working together and the common task which matter here. A children's treehouse is, or should be, a place in which children can roam freely amongst branches and leaves without constant monitoring by parents. This is a place where they can build extensions or redesign without following their parents' instructions. A treehouse can also be a place dedicated to the entire family.

TREEHOUSES IN LITERATURE, FILM, AND COMIC

THE BARON IN THE TREES

Humans living in trees seldom appear in literature. One distinguished example is provided by Italo Calvino's philosophical, fantastical novel *The Baron in the Trees*. After quarrelling with his tyrannical father, the book's twelve-year-old hero, Cosimo, climbs a holm oak in their garden and declares: 'I'm never coming down again'. The young Baron spends the rest of his life in the trees and never again sets foot on earth. As a fire watchman and specialist of cutting fruit trees for the construction of aqueducts, he wanders through the treetops, making himself useful. Calvino describes in detail how Cosimo hunts in the trees and wanders from Italy to Spain, without touching the ground. In the novel, the reader has only a vague idea of how the protagonist lived in the trees prior to his death at age 65. At the beginning of the book, Cosimo's brother Biagio, four years younger, describes 'a little chamber' through which the trunk of a beech passes, surrounded by tents and carpets. The floor is made of planks and thick branches. Biagio doubts whether this structure is balanced. Cosimo explains to him that this housing is provisional and that he still needs to 'thoroughly study' the art of building houses in trees. In the further course of the novel, Cosimo spends some time sleeping like a silkworm in a cocoon, such as when he fastens a sleeping bag padded with fur to one of the tree's branches. Later, he finds a new love nest for himself and his adored Viola in the seashell-shaped hollow of a nut tree trunk, which he covers with the skin of a wild boar. The novel, which first appeared in 1957, immerses the reader in the world of trees in a highly poetic manner, and is a wonderful read for every treehouse inhabitant.

TARZAN – THE LORD OF THE JUNGLE

The character of Tarzan, dreamt up by the American writer Edgar Rice Burroughs in the early years of the 20th century, is arguably the world's best known tree dweller. The first story, published in a pulp magazine in 1912, was followed shortly afterwards by the first book with numerous episodes. The story conquered magazines, the world of comics and, finally, the silver screen. Tarzan was filmed with famous actors such as Elmo Lincoln (1918 silent film), Johnny Weissmüller, Maureen O'Sullivan and Lex Barker. In *Tarzan the Ape Man*, filmed in 1932 with Johnny Weissmüller in the title role, Tarzan lived in various places high up in the treetops. His house stands on protruding forks of branches and is turned into a little nest, lined with leopard skins. Tarzan kidnaps the beautiful Jane and takes her to one of these deerstands – against her will at first. In the film *Tarzan Escapes* from 1936 with the same leading actor, the housing is more comfortable. The treehouse of the two protagonists now has six rooms. Running water, a fireplace, and technical fittings such as ventilators are in evidence. A rope bridge connects the main house to an annexe with further rooms. The elephant-operated lift is a wonderful touch.

MARSUPILAMI

Marsupilami is a comic book and cartoon film animal, vaguely reminiscent of a leopard. He lives in a treehouse fastened to the tree with lianas. Created by André Franquin, it is one of the most famous Franco-Belgian cartoon characters.

THE SIMPSONS

In the cartoon series *The Simpsons*, Bart's treehouse serves as a hideout for himself and his best friend, Milhouse, and is a place where they can think up new pranks. It is situated behind his parents' house in the fictional town of Springfield, and was also temporarily converted into a casino and a junior Playboy Mansion. For each series of *The Simpsons*, several horror episodes known as the Treehouse of Horror were produced and screened at Halloween.

ANIMALS

Animals are surely the real masters of treehouse architecture.

THE TREE AND THE TREEHOUSE

KLAUS SCHÖPE

TREES – GIANTS WITH A HISTORY

Trees can look back at a very long history. Long before the first anthropoid creatures appeared on the face of the earth, there were already trees. Perhaps trees will still be here when the last human has disappeared. Coniferous trees, as we know them today, have already been around for 160 million years. Deciduous trees, on the other hand, are younger – dating back 65 million years. The ginkgo, the oldest known living species of tree, can proudly claim to have existed on our planet for 290 million years. Those who become involved with trees should always bear one thing in mind: Trees deserve respect due to their venerable past. Their ability to demonstrate stability despite external changes can be relied upon. Over the course of their existence they have developed strategies to overcome difficulties.

THE DEVELOPMENT OF TREES

In the battle for light, air, and nutrients, trees have asserted themselves over other plants. Around 330 million years ago, the scale tree (lepidodendron), already possessed a stable system in the shape of rind, comprising 99 percent cork. However, cork is not very stable, which meant these trees which reached a height of 30 metres with a diameter of five metres, wasted their material. Only gradually did wood develop to bear the weight. Wood lasted for many years and withstood the test of time. The wood in the trunk and branches is more resistant to wind and other environmental influences than bark. Thus, the proportion of bark in the trunk reduced and the trees became slender. The first step in the development of the tree was its upward growth, without branches. It then began to spread horizontally, developing branches and crown. In the battle for light, trees use two different strategies:

_01. The conqueror:
      rapidly growing wood which neglects its
      static safety and does not live very long
_02. The stalwart:
      slower growing wood with better static
      properties, which attains a greater age

Growth is caused by primary stimulation. Upward growth is instigated by the growth stimulant, phototropism, which means bending towards light. In addition, growth is regulated by chemotropism, the urge for food, and by geotropism, the plant's response to gravity. Thus, each tree tries to orient its trunk vertically towards the centre of the earth. It grows with one shoot pointing vertically upwards, away from the centre of the earth, with its roots growing towards it. Growth is steered by plant hormones – 'auxins'. With greater concentrations of this growth substance on the underside of the shoot, the stalk curls upwards while the root enclosed in the earth grows downwards since the lower part is inhibited in its growth. The concentration of hormones in the cells has a different effect on roots and on the stalk: What is good for the stalk is an inhibitor for the roots. Geotropism always works as follows: The tree regularly 'grows around' obstacles – assisted by phototropism. This should also be taken into consideration when planning and building houses in trees. Photosynthesis, the conversion which takes place in the plant's leaves, then creates nutrients ('assimilates' for example).

Once the tree has achieved the required orientation and conquered the aerial space it needs, the next stage of growth commences: the 'secondary thickness growth'. From this point in time, the tree focuses increasingly on expanding its girth, while upward growth slows down. Naturally, upward growth is also restricted by other factors such as the limitations of transporting water up to the tree-top. Thus, the wind generates a stimulus which encourages the tree to grow. Growth hormones are dispersed, which cause growth in those areas most at risk. In a young tree, this will be the entire trunk, then the branches and forks, followed later by the transitional area above the soil, the root flare, etc. Once the tree has completed its main growth phase, it is considered fully grown in biological terms. From a statical viewpoint, it may be seen as fully grown once it has achieved around two-thirds of its potential size. In Europe, most trees are between 20 and 30 metres high, and are therefore all of a similar size. Naturally, there are also the giants, which grow to heights of 40 metres and more. That in turn depends on general conditions and locations. On the other hand, in different parts of the world trees can achieve heights of up to 150 metres – in that case, however, not even the strongest tree can guarantee that water will be transported from root to crown: Such tremendous suction places enormous pressure on the tree. The development of the wood inside the tree varies from species to species. The differences in the wood are relevant, for example, in the case of fungal damage, when each tree responds in a different way, compensating for the damage in a different manner and stabilising itself at a faster or slower rate. In growing, the tree's own weight increases and it is exposed to higher wind speeds: The wind pressure on the crown of a tree almost quadruples when the wind's speed doubles. At the same time, the tree's resilience and stability increase at a greater rate: With the doubling of the tree's girth, its stability increases eightfold. In the case of normal development, the tree has sufficient time to achieve adequate thickness, thus increasing its safety reserves. However, 'group pressure' can inhibit this development and restrict thickness growth. Particularly in the case of later injuries, the tree needs to be able to fall back on these reserves.

A TREE AS A LIVING, LOAD-BEARING STRUCTURE

MARTIN ZELLER

Trees consist of visible organs, such as the trunk, branches, twigs and leaves, and underground organs integrated in the root system that are not visible to us. Strong roots are responsible for stability, fine roots and symbiotic mycorrhizal fungi are responsible for the supply of water and minerals.

Trees are living organisms that grow from germination to death, metabolise, ward off diseases and parasites, have sensory organs and are therefore able to respond to external stimuli.

Stability and robustness of a tree are not primarily programmed by the tree species, but by the processing of these external stimuli. Influences of forces coming from wind, rain and snow produce growth which is significant for the specific location. For example, a pine tree in an exposed position may produce a greater density of wood than an oak tree in a nutrient-rich and sheltered position.

In conventional construction, micro houses are connected to the ground by supports and foundations. In treehouse construction the trunk and the root system of the load-bearing tree perform this task. In conventional construction, deterioration begins from completion of the supporting structure by corrosion, abrasion, and physical decomposition.

In treehouse construction it is very different: the vital supporting tree is able to adapt loads led in and optimise itself accordingly by forming reaction wood. A brief explanation: vital trees dispose of receptors able to detect locally increased stresses in core and root system after the installation of a treehouse. In order to return to the former stress level (stress = force / surface), the cross-sectional surface will be increased by radial thickness growth. In addition, a vital tree is able to produce special wood material through cell differentiation,

which has means of more tensile strength or more compressive strength depending on the direction of stress.

For defending diseases, the vital tree has various tools at hand: microorganisms and parasites are repelled by scents and hormones, invading individuals are fought under usage of tree sap and resin. Wood-decomposing fungi are biochemically sealed off in compartments so that they cannot spread further in the wood core.

The striking difference between a technical supporting structure and a vital tree as a load-bearing structure is obvious: while a technical supporting structure is exposed to deterioration from beginning on, a vital tree as a living load-bearing structure optimises its shape and material and, in addition, operates an active defence against diseases and parasites.

CHOOSING THE PROPER TREE FOR A TREEHOUSE

To ensure that a selected tree is also suitable as a load-bearing tree for a treehouse, several detailed investigations are required. Those will be carried out after a biological and morphological assessment, in which the basic suitability as a possible load-bearing tree is determined. In the regulations on tree assessment a distinction between visual assessment and further examinations is described. For trees along streets and in public parks further investigations must be carried out only if the preceding visual assessment reveals indications of an impairment of stability and/or fracture resistance.

For an assessment of trees that are subjected to carry artificial loads in addition to natural loads (for example, due to the installation of a high ropes course or a treehouse), relevant regulations require proof of sufficient load-bearing capacity. For good reason: the previously unloaded tree is initially weakened in its stability and resistance to fracture

by the additional load. In the subsequent adaptation phase a vital tree develops appropriate reaction wood to absorb all initially excessive stresses. As described earlier, only the above-ground parts of a tree are visible to us, although the invisible components, i.e. the root system, play a significant role in its suitability as a load-bearing tree. A purely visual assessment is insufficient because of this reason. A proper calculation and proof test are required.

SAFETY CHECK LEVEL 1 - VISUAL TREE ASSESSMENT

First general suitability of the selected tree species is checked. Not every tree species is suitable for bearing artificial loads. Moreover, some tree species do react protectively when contacted by artificial attachments. Very suitable tree species are beech, maple, oak, cedar, silver fir and giant

sequoia. Mechanical problems can occur with, for example, sweet chestnut, red oak, Scottish pine and spruce. Physiological problems can occur with, for example, birch species which includes hornbeam, linden, poplar, and horse chestnut. The general suitability is primarily determined by the extent of the wood core density changing after mechanical intervention and how well a tree species is able to repel invading fungi and parasites. In addition, the effects of climate change must also be considered. Of course, morphology of a tree is relevant for an arrangement with a treehouse, too.

In the second step of the visual tree assessment, the potential load-bearing tree is examined for externally perceptible signs of disease. A possible infestation with wood decomposing fungi (tree rots or decay), parasites, bacteria or other microorganisms should also be recognised by a qualified tree expert.

SAFETY CHECK LEVEL 2 - FURTHER INVESTIGATIONS

For further investigations, more or less complex tools and equipment are required such as probing rods, soft-face hammers, punches, endoscope cameras, drilling resistance measuring devices, sonic or electric tomographs, etc. As with other living beings on our planet, there is no one hundred percent perfect tree existing. A healthy infestation with parasites and a symbiosis with certain bacteria and fungi is not a criteria for exclusion, but completely natural and therefore acceptable. However, a diseased tree, which looses vitality and/or stability due to the infestation, is ruled out as a load-bearing tree.

Tree assessment level 2 – further investigations of potential load-bearing trees – is also very different from further investigations on street and park trees, where the restriction of stability and/ or breakage safety is accepted to a certain extent. Above all, morphological and mechanical damage can quickly disqualify a selected tree as a load-bearing tree. For example, bark inclusion or decay in the wood core cannot be accepted at all in a load-bearing tree, because they represent predetermined breaking areas. In the event of damage

or accident, no insurance company would compensate financially if it was assessed that the supporting structure was mechanically pre-damaged.

SAFETY CHECK LEVEL 3 - TREE ENGINEERING REPORT

In traditional construction, a structural analysis of the supporting structure and the foundation is required by law. It is only logical that a corresponding analysis has to be carried out for the calculation of the load-bearing capacity of a living tree that shall serve as a supporting structure for a treehouse. Because there is no industrial standard existing for this verification, both the authorities and the responsible tree experts are currently struggling with a suitable form of static and dynamic verification.

The Tree Engineering Report describes and evaluates a potential support tree, explains its function in the surrounding forest, its morphology and the expected load capacity. Depending on the design of the treehouse and its access, different connecting techniques should be recommended. All parameters for the load side, i.e. all forces acting on the living tree caused by the proposed

treehouse, wind and traffic are listed. The parameters for the resistance side are determined by laboratory testing of a core sample. These are the compressive, tensile and flexural strengths of the individual tree. As stated, trees in different locations develop widely varying strengths. Therefore, it is not possible to work with generally valid tables in this situation. In order to compare and balance the resistance of a supporting tree with the load side, its individual values must be known. Finally, taking into account an appropriate safety factor, the reference value against a possible tree failure can be calculated very precisely.

With the Tree Engineering Report, the undersigning tree engineer assumes liability for the operational safety of the supporting tree, or the supporting trees if it is a complex installation. Under the term 'Tree Management', further advice is provided on tree, nature and environmental protection in this report. Regulation of traffic by means of suitable routing should be emphasised, too. The area around load-bearing trees should be kept free of traffic to avoid soil compaction. Above all, the non-visible part of each tree, the root system, is a vital and very sensitive organ that needs special protection.

TREE ENGINEERING

Tree Engineering is a relatively new science that encompasses the biology, morphology, mechanics, statics and dynamics of trees and provides statical analysis of load-bearing trees by using Finite Elements Methods (FEM).

In addition to its primary objective (anchoring technical installations in vital and sufficiently load-bearing trees) Tree Engineering also pursues goals of sustainable construction as well as climate protection through the creation or preservation of forests, while providing living and working space. Tree Engineering is a field of work in civil engineering; it addresses subjects in both civil engineering and architecture. This also includes planning and construction of the technical installation which is anchored in sufficiently vital trees. In the overall system, the 'load-bearing tree' or 'support tree' mainly assumes the functions of primary support structure and foundation at the same time. Supporting trees often take over other functions, such as external climatic regulation: in summer, the leafy supporting tree provides shade for the treehouse; in winter, sunlight can fall unhindered through the non-leafy crown and provides passive solar energy.

The Tree Engineering Assessment Report plays an important role in Tree Engineering. In this document, individual statically relevant parameters of the tree are recorded and interpreted, which forms the basis for all further planning. In the Tree Engineering Assessment Report, the load-bearing capacity of the living tree is compared mathematically with the load inputs delivered by the stress analyst. In this respect, Tree Engineering also plays an important role in public traffic safety. The aim here is to reliably determine and document the stability and breakage safety of a tree in public space. On this basis of mechanical considerations, decisions can be made about further measures, such as pruning, crown stabilisation, guiding, bracing, etc.

Tree Engineering courses are offered for students by the Faculty of Architecture and Civil Engineering at the Technical University of Dortmund. As professional training for arboriculturists and tree inspectors, state-sponsored courses are held at the Kaiserstuhl Tree Center (Baumzentrum Kaiserstuhl). The most important contents of a Tree Engineering training are tree anatomy and growth principles, laboratory investigation of green woods, reaction behaviour of a tree due to statically relevant changes and the development of calculation models for the statics and dynamics of the load-bearing tree, as well as its dynamic interaction with the treehouse or any other technical installation.

In order to collect scientific data, proof tests are carried out at TU Dortmund University on 'green wood', which differs strikingly in strength from technically dried timber. In a test facility, whole tree trunks can be mechanically examined. At the same time, research is being carried out in nature to record the dynamics of living trees under different morphological conditions under usage of accelerometers. All datas collected are the basis of further Finite Elements Analysis (FEA).

ATTACHMENT OF A TREEHOUSE

LEARNING FROM MISTAKES OF THE PAST

(1) Damages caused by Wrapping

(2) Damages caused by Clamping

(3) Damages caused by Strangulation

In principle, 5 solutions are available for connecting technical equipment or technical installations to living trees:

1. Wrapping Technique

Special care must be taken to ensure that the compression pads are elastically supported. Otherwise, massive damage to the supporting tree will occur in the medium to long term, because the increased thickness growth between the compression timbers will lead to accelerated filling of the gaps. Once this condition is reached, all the conductive pathways in and under the bark mantle are pinched off (Image 1).

Many hundreds of load-bearing trees have been killed in adventure parks and ropes courses in forests by this wrapping or slinging technique. Strangulating wrapping techniques should therefore be rejected on principle.

2. Clamping Technique

In clamping technique, load-bearing beams are clamped directly to the tree in form of single or double tongs. If pressure-absorbing viscose-elastic material is added as a stress buffer and the tongs will be regularly widened, clamping technique is justifiable.

In practice, these precautionary measures are often omitted for cost reasons, with the result that massive deformations of the tree shaft occur, up to the death of the load-bearing tree

(Image 2). For this reason, a use of the clamping technique without stress buffer and adjustment mechanism in treehouse construction should be rejected.

3. Connection with Slings

If cheap slings – not manufactured for this purpose – are used to induce loads onto a living tree, this inevitably leads to impairment of the radial thickness growth and thus to strangulation of the supporting tree (Image 3).

The use of open slings, on the other hand, is a slinging technique that is gentle on the tree and should be recommended for this reason (Image 4). Specially manufactured tree slings are now available on the market (Image 5).

4. Tree Screws, Bolts and other Connectors

Again and again, construction elements appear on the market which shall be attached to the living tree with more or less suitable screws and/or bolts. A screwed adapter plate cannot be healed over well by the supporting tree. Sometimes 'tree screws' made of non-precious materials are offered, which can poison the metabolism of the supporting tree.

5. Implantation Technology – modular, adaptive Connection Systems

Implants differ from normal tree screws mainly in three criteria: first, the force-absorbing part

of the implant (Image 6) does not rest on the outside of the bark or protrude from it, but is anchored in the wood core (Image 7). Second, the ingrowth of the implant is calculated and supported by a special thread shape with a branch-like exterior section. Third, the modular system offers extension pieces which shall be used if the radial thickness growth reaches the end of the implant. Implantation technology means to integrate a specially moulded anchor into the load-bearing tree, which has many characteristics of a natural branch connection.

A large number of tests on different tree species over a period of 13 years have proven that a vital tree easily incorporates a well-designed implant through reaction wood, the 'callus' and natural thickness growth (Image 8). If the end of the implant is reached, an extension piece can be screwed on and when the end of the extension piece is reached a second and third extension can be screwed on, too. In this way the modular implant 'grows with the tree' (Image 9).

On the subject of tree protection:

In order to proceed in a minimally invasive manner, each implant is individually dimensioned in accordance with the principle 'as small as possible, as big as necessary'. In addition, depending on the tree species, a specific stainless steel is selected to ensure that the sometimes corrosive tree sap cannot trigger a chemical reaction with the metal implant.

(4) Open Sling

(5) Professional Tree Sling

(6) Force-absorbing part of an implant

(7) Incorporation of an implant

(8) Natural dead-brach connection

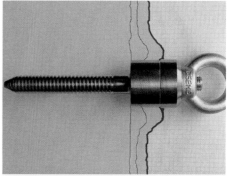

(9) Implant with an extension part

AN INDUSTRIAL STANDARD FOR TREEHOUSES?

When asked this question, every creative planner of a treehouse is sure to shake his head as a spontaneous reaction. But that's a misunderstanding! Well-drafted standards do not restrict freedom of design, but merely set criteria for a minimum level of safety. On the DIN (German Institute of Standardisation) homepage one can read: 'Alternative forms of housing such as tiny houses and treehouses are increasing in demand and are thus coming more and more into the focus of building supervisory authorities, who are asking for a basis for an evaluation of such structural facilities.' The big advantage of standardisation is therefore clear: compliance with a corresponding industrial standard will provide evidence of a minimum standard for product safety in the building application procedure for tiny houses and treehouses. A simplified procedure can be used to obtain a building permit quickly. This industrial standard is currently in development.

PROJECTS
-
2003–2021

TREEHOUSE PLENDELHOF

BASSUM NEAR BREMEN, GERMANY

-

2003 / THE FIRST TREEHOUSE

As a child, I never had my own treehouse. I enjoyed climbing trees and my friends and I would build other constructions, such as huts and little dams. Therefore, it was quite some time before I came up with the idea, as an adult, to design and build a treehouse.

Having completed a carpentry apprenticeship, studied architecture and gained several years of professional experience, my love of building had not disappeared – although I had lost the innocent and spontaneous approach of my childhood. The idea of designing, building, and then using a little space high up in a tree was most appealing. During my studies and my work as an architect, I had always been inspired and influenced by experimental building culture. Therefore, I was keen to develop a contemporary interpretation for the treehouse. The question of how a built structure should be anchored in a living organism was entirely new to me. When designing a treehouse, how does one handle the tree's growth and strong movement, for example in a storm? Before I could explore these issues, I first had to find the right place with suitable trees. Luckily, some friends offered me the opportunity to undertake this unusual project on their property. The environment of the riding stables was perfect: a well-equipped workshop, a beautiful landscape, and, most importantly, some large, healthy trees. Having quickly chosen two magnificent beeches I was ready to start designing. What I wanted to do was create a space which, even in a small area, would provide adequate room for a couple of friends to gather together comfortably. Naturally, it should also be possible for two people to sleep there. Another important point was a south-facing sun deck, on which one could sit directly under the leaves in summer. Now the crucial question of how to fasten the construction to the trees needed to be answered. After various conversations with respected arborists, the best idea seemed to be to suspend the treehouse from the trees with flexible connectors. By using highly resilient textile straps, the trees would be able to move freely in the wind.

TREEHOUSE
PLENDELHOF

BASSUM NEAR BREMEN, GERMANY
-
2003

❦ The design concept for the treehouse entailed building the closed part and the terrace in a single connected unit, and suspending it between the two trees. A few preliminary sketches produced a slender, boatlike structure with a triangular floor plan. The proposed means of access was via a vertical and a diagonal staircase.

After climbing nine metres up the beeches, one would enter the treehouse via a hatch in the floor. Light and good vision were also important design criteria. Long, horizontal tilting windows on the side walls, a roof hatch, and the horizontally glazed tip of the treehouse would offer an almost all-round view of the crown and the surrounding meadows. Creature comforts are provided by a small heating unit, soft cushions and mattresses, interior and outside lighting, and a small hi-fi system. Once the design was in place, the construction of the treehouse got underway in summer. Over the following months, a disused barn on the estate was used as an assembly hall. It was here that the entire treehouse was prepared. The mounting of the treehouse cabin onto the prepared substructure was then undertaken after the winter break with the help of a few friends and a small truck-mounted crane. After this exciting and, at times, extremely exhausting building phase, my first treehouse was complete. Certainly, one of the most exciting moments of my life was when I climbed up for the first time, opened the floor hatch, and took in the view and the overall effect. Since its completion, this place in the trees has taken on a special importance for me and my friends. We often drink coffee or serve dinner here on the terrace. I and many of my friends and acquaintances have spent highly atmospheric nights here in this special place in the trees, both in summer and winter. At the time, I had not expected that my first treehouse would lead to a whole new area of activity, and that, using the *Baumraum* brand, I would design and build many more treehouses.

TREES	-	two beeches
HEIGHT	-	9.1 m
STATICS	-	suspension by means of steel cable and textile straps to two beeches
BEARING STRUCTURE	-	untreated larch
TERRACE	-	5.4 sqm
INTERIOR AREA	-	7.6 sqm
FAÇADE CONSTRUCTION	-	from inside to outside: 20 mm spruce boarding, raw (recycled); spruce framework 60/60 mm, filled with insulating material; wind foil, black; 20 mm air space; 20 mm untreated, horizontal larch boarding

TREEHOUSE WENCKE

NESSE NEAR BREMERHAVEN, GERMANY

-

2004

This treehouse for a married couple and their three children was the first commercial project which was undertaken by *Baumraum* for a client. The client's property is at the edge of the village of Nesse, near Bremerhaven, in Lower Saxony. The length of the large garden is demarcated on one side by the house, and at the western end by a double row of various trees. Behind the trees, there is a typical North German landscape of meadows and paddocks. The spot chosen for the treehouse was at the northern end of the row of trees with two limes and two ash trees, right beside a small campfire site. Expert examination showed that three of the four trees were healthy and stable, but the smaller of the two ash trees was damaged and unsuitable for bearing additional loads. The basic concept of this project was similar to that of the 'Treehouse Plendelhof' – here too the treehouse cabin would be built together with the terrace, and then lifted into the trees using a truck-mounted crane. The treehouse structure stood on four beams which were fastened to the trees by means of steel cables and textile straps.

TREEHOUSE
WENCKE

NESSE NEAR BREMERHAVEN,
GERMANY
-
2004

TREEHOUSE
WENCKE

NESSE NEAR BREMERHAVEN, GERMANY
-
2004

The treehouse achieves its striking form thanks to the angular construction elements on a conically-shaped base. One enters the treehouse via a ladder and floor hatch. The interior design and space-saving furnishings are reminiscent of the cosy comfort aboard a boat. Beneath the divan area and the bench, each member of the family has a pull-out box – two of which can also be used as tables. The two horizontal window wings, a large, diagonal glassed area at the end of the bed, and the skylight allow plenty of sun to enter the treehouse. A vertical window separates the sitting area inside from the identically aligned terrace bench, and provides a charming view from the inside to the outside. An angularly-shaped door opening leads to the spacious treehouse terrace. Here the visitor is protected from wind and rain.

TREES	- two ashes and two limes
HEIGHT	- 3.8 m
STATICS	- suspension by means of steel cable and textile straps to four trees
TERRACE	- untreated larch
INTERIOR AREA	- 8.6 sqm
TERRACE AREA	- 7.3 sqm
FAÇADE CONSTRUCTION	- from inside to outside: 20 mm larch boarding, tongue and groove, spruce framework 60/60 mm, filled with mineral insulation; wind foil; 20 mm air space; 20 mm untreated, horizontal larch boarding

TREEHOUSE
LAKE TEGERN

COMMUNITY WARNGAU, GERMANY
-
2004

The word 'idyllic' immediately springs to mind when one sees the Bavarian alpine uplands. Farmhouses with richly ornamented façades and heavy, broadly overhanging roofs are the hallmarks of the local architecture. Cows wearing bells graze in lush meadows, while crystal clear mountain streams and lakes warm the heart. Farmers in traditional costume sit on tractors and, in the distance, one can see the first tips of the Alps thrusting skyward majestically. Perhaps this image is a stereotype but here, a few kilometres north of Lake Tegern, all of the features described are in evidence.

The clients live with their four children in a big German city, which is the complete opposite to this idyll for most of the year. During the school holidays the family members avail of the benefits offered by their Bavarian country home to enjoy everything they have been missing in the city – endless space for the children to play, fresh air, and, in winter, skiing in the mountains. Naturally, there are plenty of beautiful trees which are perfect for climbing and in which one might also consider building a treehouse. In keeping with old tradition, such an undertaking can be carried out by the children themselves.

TREES	one ash
HEIGHT	depending on the hillside position between 3.5 m and 5 m
STATICS	suspension by means of steel cable and textile straps to one ash
TERRACE	untreated larch
INTERIOR AREA	6.4 sqm
TERRACE AREA	7.9 sqm
FAÇADE CONSTRUCTION	from inside to outside: 20 mm larch boarding, tongue and groove, untreated; 20 mm plywood; 60 mm wood wool insulation; wind foil; 20 mm air space; 22 mm weather boarding of untreated larch
ROOFING	larch shingles

PEAR TREEHOUSE

HEILBRONN, GERMANY

–

2005

The property known as the 'Äckerle' is situated on the edge of Heilbronn, surrounded by orchards and vineyards. The large garden's name has a long history and reveals its Swabian origins. The treehouse was a gift from the client to her husband and was to be integrated into a large pear tree at the western end of the property. The client also wanted a comfortable staircase and a spacious terrace. The treehouse's design is characterised by a dynamic vocabulary and a spiral-shaped arrangement of the main construction elements around the old fruit tree. The stairs, terrace and front part of the treehouse cabin are completely attached to the tree by means of flexible hangers. Two conically-shaped stabiliser links secure the rear part of the treehouse and ensure that the pear tree is not overloaded. Stairs lead to the main terrace, 3.5 m above the ground.

PEAR
TREEHOUSE

HEILBRONN, GERMANY
-
2005

❧ At the special request of the client, part of the terrace can be dropped so that practice golf balls can be hit from here to the adjacent lawn area. A small staircase leads to the treehouse cabin.

PEAR TREEHOUSE

HEILBRONN, GERMANY
-
2005

The construction, made of indigenous larch, is insulated on all sides and fitted with an upholstered sleeping and seating area. None of the wall or ceiling surfaces are at right angles to each other. The windows on the southwest side are equipped with sunshade elements and prevent the small room from overheating. At the end of the bed area the corner is generously glazed, affording a view of the vineyards in the eastern part of the valley – a spellbinding sight which the viewer can easily wax lyrical about.

TREES	-	a pear tree
HEIGHT	-	first level: 3.5 m; second level: 4.5 m
STATICS	-	suspension by means of steel cables and textile straps on the pear tree; part of the treehouse s weight is held by two flexibly mounted stabiliser links
TERRACE	-	untreated larch (glued wood)
INTERIOR AREA	-	8.6 sqm
TERRACE AREA	-	12.4 sqm
FAÇADE CONSTRUCTION	-	from inside to outside: 20 mm larch boarding, tongue and groove, untreated; 20 mm plywood; 60 mm mineral insulation; wind foil; 20 mm air space; 25 mm larch battens

LOOKOUT
STATION

SEEBODEN AT LAKE MILLSTATT, CARINTHIA, AUSTRIA
-
2005

❧ The 'Lookout Station' is a little gem with a big view. Our clients, a married couple from Carinthia, wanted to create a place for their large family. This was to be a special sleeping and play area for their children and eight grandchildren – a place for daydreaming and observing. The widely visible treehouse tower perches on a slope above the town of Seeboden in Austria.

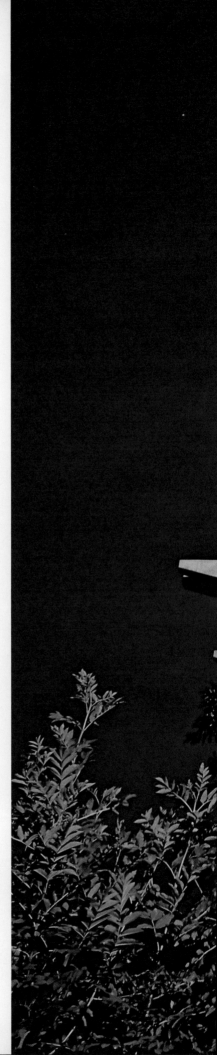

❦ Inside, there are windows on all sides. However, one's eye is immediately captivated by the view from the panorama window at the end of the large reclining area, where one can see Lake Millstatt, the boats, surrounding villages, and several mountains.

TREES	-	set between several silver firs, ashes, yews, and various bushes
HEIGHT	-	terrace: 1 to 17 m; treehouse: 2.2 m above the terrace
STATICS	-	standing framework; larch on 4 reinforced concrete pad foundations
TERRACE	-	untreated larch
INTERIOR AREA	-	8.6 sqm
TERRACE AREA	-	13.4 sqm
FAÇADE CONSTRUCTION	-	from inside to outside: 20 mm larch boarding, untreated; 60 mm mineral insulation; wind foil; 20 mm air space; 20 mm larch battens

The spaces in between

When I was still a little boy, I saw my dream house at the cinema. Tarzan was living in it. There and then I decided that, whenever I could, I would recreate that house myself. It would be high above everybody's heads in the apple tree and would be just for me. The old apple tree has long since shed the treehouse of my childhood and I am now decades older, but the feeling of standing on that little terrace between heaven and earth is just as overwhelming as it was then when I saw my first dream house. A castle in the clouds ... the primeval urge to retreat into a tree and, in a manner of speaking, get one's feet off the ground ... has remained as strong as ever. And, to be honest, I am truly happy that we now use more durable material for building than Tarzan did in his day. So, in a sense, I've remained a child and am just building a bit more – for my grandchildren – and, of course, for myself.

Removed

It is a fact that Michel Foucault's text *Of Other Spaces* has greatly influenced the discourse on space in recent decades. The philosopher says analogously that (real) places are outside of all places, even though it may be possible to indicate their location in reality.

My treehouse is also this kind of everyday antipole: As concrete as its location in a real, existing tree may be, the house itself is – in a literal sense – 'removed'; although it has no foundations, it is still firmly rooted. For me, it is the embodiment of a childhood dream of freedom and safety.

Ufo

What is more enjoyable than flying? Can one meet oneself at this altitude? And, in this unaccustomed environment, should one not carry a mobile phone to be on the safe side? Unusual thoughts up here, 17 metres above the ground which, in my case, also means 17 metres above sea level and perhaps 17 metres higher than normal. In formal terms, the object in the tree resembles an UFO, somewhat resembling a spaceship which has become entangled in the branches while attempting to land. However, these technical associations are immediately contradicted by the craftsmanlike structure and the material: weather-resistant, indigenous wood. It smells of wood – of beautifully handled wood. Completely clad in larch, the cottage's aroma is sensual. With regard to the interior, here too it is wood that sets the tone. The room is warm and welcoming, as one would expect from a retreat which withdraws into the background in sun and heat, but offers safety and warmth when it is raining

Bird flight

Lakeside tranquillity

and windy. Then the treehouse becomes a fine living space, a place for individual wellbeing. As an architectural curiosity, it is the perfect combination of artistic discrimination, design experience, and skilled craftsmanship. Inside it is furnished like a ship's cabin. Absolutely no furniture – that belongs on the ground, not in a tree! The spirit cannot grow where space is constricted by furniture. My bed in the tree is a canopy bed with a heavenly view. Particularly gazing out the roof hatch towards the branch-work in the sky immediately invites one to day-dream. Looking through a long side window beside the bed, the eye falls on a young ash which is reflected in the glass, the silver fir, and my house with its glass façade. The large panorama window at the front offers a breathtaking view of Mirnock Mountain opposite, whose perfectly formed peak is mirrored in the waters of Lake Millstatt. Thus, this room becomes a wonderful space for experiencing the landscape.

And what if I don't want to come down any more? Away from the worries about ups and downs. Up here, we're talking about more elevated things – stars, freshness, breathing, growing – my world is the treetops, roof hatch, a shooting star. The infinitely beautiful moment is over quickly ... and then black night. And I wait longingly for morning's return. What can be lovelier than to be woken gently by birdsong and the rustling of leaves? For just a moment I close my eyes again, spread my wings, listen to the wind playing, and dream ... I am the lord of the castle up here. My house in the tree lives with the tree and with me. When the wind whistles around the corners every now and then, the house creaks and sways a little – like a ship. And when there's thunder and lightning the house breathes a sigh as if it would like to shake off the inconveniences of nature, like the tree on which it stands, like a dog shaking off its wet fur. My grandchildren will now be able to see for themselves what it's like when there's lightning, or snow, or when the sun shines – in the flesh, and not just virtually. The transition between inside and outside is flowing; windows on the sides and in the roof open up the view and, if they want, the children can live like the tree. They can shrink or grow with it – freely withdraw into silence and security. And they have the choice of enjoying life in the middle of otherwise inaccessible nature. They have a place to which they can retreat and put some space between themselves and moody adults. Up here, they can think in peace, work through anger or disappointments, and cook up fresh mischief. Or they can invite friends to discuss the important aspects of life or exchange secrets – provided they don't prefer their tree to be their only confidant.

What does it smell of up here? Of trees, of Lake Millstatt, and, yes, of a childhood spent on the water. Shafts of sunlight are peeping into the window. The room is magically bathed in light. Trees reach towards the light. A glimpse of a fairy tale world ...

The view is beautiful – truly and deeply beautiful: a wide expanse of bluish green water, rowing boats, sailboats, a steamer for the summer visitors. The *Kärnten* circles the lake, with people aboard pointing: Look at this ... yes ... what's that over there? It's my treehouse.

MIRKO BOGATAJ, SEEBODEN 2005

CASA
GIRAFA

CURITIBA, BRAZIL
-
2006

Brazil makes one think of samba, and the tropical rainforest with mighty, towering trees. Everyone is inspired by this idea, particularly the treehouse builder. Naturally, the culture and landscapes of this enormous country are hugely varied. Densely populated metropolises, alongside gigantic areas of primeval forest, swamp, steppes, and, of course, the enchanting beaches, all combine to make it unique and define its diversity. Curitiba, the clients' home, has around 1.8 million inhabitants and is located in a temperate zone in the south. The four-member family recently had a modern house built by a well-known Brazilian architect and had only just moved in. The lady of the house has long been fascinated by treehouses and, by chance, had come across a *Baumraum* project in a German interiors magazine. Once the initial contact had been made, it

wasn't long before planning could start on an extravagant addition to their new residence. The property is in one of the closed residential developments with high walls and a secure driveway which are so typical of this country. On the south-facing part of the property, there is a large terrace with a pool and a couple of palms. On the northern side, on a green area enclosed by a high hedge, there are two sturdy north American maple trees. The maple in the centre of the lawn was to be the basis for the treehouse. After various model sketches were made, a concept was developed for a terrace suspended in the tree and a freestanding treehouse cabin. The load of the treehouse is transferred to a concrete foundation by nine slender, asymmetrically arranged stainless steel pillars which evoke a long-legged animal, such as a giraffe.

CASA
GIRAFA

CURITIBA, BRAZIL
-
2006

CASA
GIRAFA

CURITIBA, BRAZIL
-
2006

The terrace's weight is carefully distributed across the maple by means of thin steel cables and textile straps. A small walkway with a staircase connects the two elements and also compensates for the difference in altitude. The external surfaces are distinguished by the use of ipé, a very hard Brazilian tropical wood, and brushed stainless steel on the railings and the various mountings. Reddish jatobá wood surfaces and white imitation leather upholstery and drawer fronts define the look of the interior and are reminiscent of the furnishings in a yacht. The client specially requested that a high-quality hi-fi system and also a large flatscreen TV be integrated into the treehouse.

TREES	a maple tree
HEIGHT	terrace: 3.6 m; cabin: 4.6 m
STATICS	the terrace is suspended from the maple tree by means of stainless steel cables and textile straps; the treehouse's load rests on nine asymmetrically arranged and leaning stainless steel supports
TERRACE	ipé (a very hard wood from Brazil)
INTERIOR AREA	9.6 sqm
TERRACE AREA	11.4 sqm
FAÇADE CONSTRUCTION	from inside to outside: jatobá veneer on 10 mm plywood; 19 mm OSB; 60 mm mineral insulation; membrane; 20 mm air space; 20 mm ipé boarding, horizontal

TREEHOUSE EILENRIEDE

HANOVER, GERMANY
-
2006

☙ This treehouse is in a park-like garden with many trees directly adjacent to the inner city recreational area of Eilenriede in Hanover. Only a fence separates the property, which contains a villa built in the 1920s, from the public park. In drawing up the design, our aim was to place the treehouse in a prominent position in the garden and to ensure that it afforded good views. At the same time, the construction was to be as inconspicuous as possible and hidden amongst greenery, away from the eyes of the public. The intention was that the treehouse would be supported by the trees themselves, without additional supports. The framework for this design is based on a radial footprint on two levels. The upper, fan-shaped terrace area and the slanting treehouse are held by two trees using cable constructions. While the oak is enclosed within the terrace, the hornbeam is freestanding. The interior comprises a reclining area for children, a bench opposite and a folding table. The reclining and sitting areas, as well as the cushions, are covered with wool felt. Beneath these are pull-out boxes made of dark, laminated plywood. All sides of the treehouse cabin are glazed, so that children and adults have a lovely view of the adjacent woodlands and can observe those jogging in the park without being seen themselves.

TREES	- an oak and a hornbeam
HEIGHT	- first level: 3.2 m; second level: 4.2 m
STATICS	- suspended by means of steel cables and textile straps on the oak and hornbeam
TERRACE	- untreated larch
INTERIOR AREA	- 7.8 sqm
TERRACE AREA	- downstairs: 6.4 sqm; upstairs: 8.9 sqm
FAÇADE CONSTRUCTION	- from inside to outside: 20 mm larch boarding, untreated; 60 mm mineral insulation; wind foil; 20 mm air space; 25 mm bias-cut larch battens, horizontal

BETWEEN ALDER AND OAK

BAD ROTHENFELDE NEAR
OSNABRÜCK, GERMANY
-

2006

❦ The landscape east of Osnabrück is largely typical of North Germany: fields, meadows, little woods, and no mountains to block one's view into the distance. The benefits of the landscape in Lower Saxony were combined in a particularly attractive way on the client's property and those in the neighbouring area. Despite a wide range of options, the client immediately favoured a specific place for the treehouse – beside a small stream, which runs between an alder and a mighty, crooked oak. The space between the two trees, which grew together to form a 'V', provided the ideal frame for this project. The client requested that the treehouse cabin be open to the southwest, so that there would be a view of the broad meadow and tree landscape. The most striking element of the design is the semicircular treehouse with large expanses of glass and windows. The terraces on different levels with marked longitudinal alignment are integrated into the living organism of the oak and are penetrated by its branches. On the upper level is a bench – a picturesque spot for musing and experiencing the change of the seasons at close range.

BETWEEN ALDER AND OAK

BAD ROTHENFELDE NEAR OSNABRÜCK, GERMANY
-
2006

🐛 The interior, furnished with untreated oak, comprises a spacious bed area, bench, several large pull-out boxes and a flat sideboard. Bed and bench are covered with light-grey wool felt. Several cushions complement the decor. Thanks to the all-round insulation and a small heater, the treehouse is also an ideal retreat in the winter months.

TREES	-	an oak and an alder
HEIGHT	-	terrace: 4 m; treehouse and upper terrace: 5 m
STATICS	-	suspension from the oak by means of stainless steel cables and textile straps; the greater part of the treehouse s weight rests on three conically-shaped sloping supports
TERRACE	-	native oak
INTERIOR AREA	-	9.6 sqm
FAÇADE CONSTRUCTION	-	from inside to outside: 20 mm oak boarding, untreated: 60 mm wood and steel frames with mineral insulation; wind foil; 20 mm air space; rounded oak battens 25/44 mm

TREEHOUSE LOUISA

FRANKFURT / MAIN, GERMANY

–

2007

🌿 'Louisa' is the historic name of a private park in Frankfurt-Sachsenhausen. It therefore seemed only natural to give the new treehouse this poetic name. Extensive gardens with large villas and old trees are typical of this elegant Frankfurt district.

In the clients' garden with its many trees, the treehouse could have been sited in any one of several different places. The decision was made to locate it in a large, well-sized beech on a hill, within clear eyeshot of the main house.

TREES	a beech
HEIGHT	first level: 3.5 m; second level: 4.5 m; viewing platform: 7.8 m
STATICS	suspension from the beech by means of steel cables and textile straps; part of the weight rests on two flexibly mounted stabiliser supports
TERRACE	untreated larch
INTERIOR AREA	9.6 sqm
TERRACE AREA	16.4 sqm
FAÇADE CONSTRUCTION	from inside to outside: 20 mm larch boarding, tongue and groove, untreated; rounded steel frame with flanking wooden arches of glued wood; 60 mm mineral insulation; 20 mm fir boarding; rubber sealing; 20 mm air space; larch shingles

SCOUT TREEHOUSE ALMKE

ALMKE NEAR WOLFSBURG, GERMANY
-
2007

The young members of the Association of Christian Scouts (VCP) from Wolfsburg had taken on a project which was highly ambitious in a number of senses: They wanted to create a place in which a large number of scouts could assemble, where one could come into contact with nature and also celebrate – in other words, a large treehouse for both sleeping and cooking. The treehouse was to be built on the Almke Camping Site near Wolfsburg. It was also intended that the energetic hands of the young people themselves would be used to construct this sanctuary. *Baumraum* was contracted to design the treehouse and plan its construction. Before construction could start, the scouts acquired numerous sponsors and the assistance of local institutions, without which the project could never have been implemented. The treehouse was built with the support of the Wolfsburg Youth Council (Stadtjugendring) and regional craftsmen.

SCOUT TREEHOUSE ALMKE

ALMKE NEAR WOLFSBURG, GERMANY
-
2007

The design comprises two treehouses facing each other on different levels, connected by a large terrace. A sturdy pine runs through the terrace area. The lower treehouse is used for sleeping and has space for eight people. The upper treehouse is a place where guests come together and is fitted with cooking equipment, a large dining table and a wood-burning stove for the chillier times of the year. Both treehouses have slightly vaulted roofs and are almost identical in construction. The main differences lie in the way the windows are arranged and the furnishings. The scouts' treehouse is reached by means of a sturdy, double staircase.

The young people of the Association of Christian Scouts from Wolfsburg have, with a little support, produced a great achievement of which they can truly be proud. In carrying out this project they have gathered a great deal of positive experience and created a beautiful place amongst the trees for themselves and their guests.

TREES	-	a pine
HEIGHT	-	first level: 4 m; second level: 5 m
STATICS	-	standing framework of untreated larch; six triangular supports on reinforced concrete pad foundations
TERRACE	-	untreated larch
INTERIOR AREA	-	two treehouse cabins, each with an area of 9.8 sqm
TERRACE AREA	-	15.4 sqm
FAÇADE CONSTRUCTION	-	from inside to outside: 20 mm larch boarding, untreated; 60 mm mineral insulation; wind foil; 20 mm air space; 25 mm larch battens, horizontal

MEDITATION TREEHOUSE

LAGO DI BRACCIANO NEAR ROME, ITALY
-
2007

Lago di Bracciano is just a few kilometres from the gates of Rome. For the Romans, this charmingly located lake, which is within easy reach, is a perfect recreational area. The backdrop, with its wooded mountain slopes and range of tourist amenities, is somewhat reminiscent of the great lakes on the edge of the Alps in North Italy. The area is well known for its wide range of culinary specialities such as game, wild mushrooms, and sweet chestnuts. The client's property is only accessible via narrow roads and an unpaved, sand-strewn driveway. The extensive property comprises slightly hilly meadows, a house and a few agricultural buildings. What makes this property special, however, is the chestnut grove on its eastern edge: around two dozen ancient trees with gnarled bark form an impressive backdrop. In early autumn, tons of chestnuts are harvested and processed into a wide range of delicacies. Now this place is to be functionally expanded. The client had long toyed with the idea of having a treehouse built for herself. The idea was that this space would provide a place for her and her friends to meditate.

MEDITATION
TREEHOUSE

The treehouse's design is based on a clear, straightforward design. The closed area and the terrace have a square footprint. Both sections are on the same level and are reached via a single staircase. Beneath the cube of the treehouse, there are two supports which bear most of the load. On the other hand, the chestnut tree bears the weight of the terrace and the front part of the treehouse by means of steel cables and textile straps. The framework and the terrace are made of untreated larch. For the façade, a very hard tropical wood, tatajuba, which has a reddish brown colouring, was used. The large windows reach down to the floor, allowing a smooth transition between the interior and exterior. The glassed roof also provides plenty of light as well as a view of the tree's crown. Only the east façade, with its narrow window slit, is of relatively inconspicuous design. White walls and dark flooring of oiled jatobá wood are used for the interior and underline the straightforward design. The furnishings comprise only a simple bench area and many cushions upon which the treehouse visitors can make themselves comfortable to meditate.

TREES	- a chestnut tree
HEIGHT	- treehouse and terrace: 4 m
STATICS	- around 65 % of the treehouse load rests on two supports; the smaller part of the treehouse and the terrace are suspended from the chestnut by means of steel cables and textile straps
TERRACE	- untreated larch
INTERIOR FLOORING	- jatobá solid wood flooring, oiled
INTERIOR AREA	- 14.6 sqm
TERRACE AREA	- 16 sqm
FAÇADE CONSTRUCTION	- from inside to outside: 11 mm plasterboard, cream laminated; 22 mm OSB; 60 mm mineral insulation; wind foil; 20 mm air space; 20 mm horizontal tatajuba boarding

TREEHOUSE APULIA

AVETRANA, SOUTH ITALY

-

2007

The client, who lives and works in Milan, owns a property close to the town of Avetrana in the Italian province of Apulia, where he and his family spend their holidays. The property's immediate vicinity to the sea is a highly valued quality, particularly during the hot summer months. The client wanted a treehouse to create additional sleeping space and offer the family a place for playing and relaxing.

During the first site visit in the winter before assembly, the property revealed itself to be extensive with sandy soil and countless pines. Because there were many places in which the treehouse could be sited, a thorough inspection of the property was required. The place finally chosen was the property's highest point with two gnarled pines close to the swimming pool. After a few sketches, it was agreed that the treehouse would have a two-level terrace with a right-angled design. The overlapping treehouse cabin would be on the upper level. The main loads of the construction would be transferred to the two pines by means of hangers. Since one of the trees was of a somewhat weaker structure and would have been unable to bear the projected loads, the treehouse was supported by two beams.

TREEHOUSE
APULIA

AVETRANA, SOUTH ITALY
-
2007

Inside, there is a spacious reclining area with a bench opposite. Both areas are upholstered and covered with wool felt. The generous glazing and the skylight offer a panoramic view of the gently rolling South Italian landscape and the surrounding tree-tops.

TREES	- two pines
HEIGHT	- first level: 3.2 m; second level: 4.2 m
STATICS	- suspension from the pines by means of steel cables and textile straps; part of the treehouse's weight rests on two flexibly mounted stabiliser supports
TERRACE	- untreated larch
INTERIOR AREA	- 8.8 sqm
TERRACE AREA	- downstairs 15.4 sqm; upstairs 4.9 sqm
FAÇADE CONSTRUCTION	- from inside to outside: 20 mm larch boarding, untreated; 60 mm insulation or solid wood frame; wind foil; 20 mm air space; 25 mm larch battens

NUT
ROOM

DÜSSELDORF, GERMANY
-
2007

| NUT | = | ROOM |

An old walnut tree, full of life and of strikingly attractive size, stands at the rear of a terrace house property in the Düsseldorf district of Oberkassel. It is the perfect spot for a treehouse. A design for this space in the nut tree was quickly devised, but the construction work could not start so quickly: Building regulations can be very strict in this kind of inner-city location. Owing to the close proximity of the neighbours' properties, their approval was required before this little project could go ahead – thus, good powers of persuasion were called for. Thanks to the client's charm, two of the neighbours agreed to allow a reduction in the statutory distance between properties. However, because the neighbour on the eastern side did not give his permission, the originally planned size of the terrace had to be reduced. Once these time-consuming but not insignificant details were taken care of, the building permit was issued. Before it could be placed in the tree, the structure had to be lifted over the terrace house with a large truck-mounted crane, making it necessary to block off the entire street. The prefabricated treehouse was then rolled to the tree, where it was brought into position using a trestle and a hoist. To ensure that the treehouse only subjected the walnut tree to minor loads, an independent static system was chosen for the treehouse. The rounded treehouse rests on eight slender, asymmetrically arranged stainless steel supports. Thanks to the arrangement of the supports, which appears accidental, the construction somewhat resembles a large insect on the forest floor. The terrace is one metre lower and held in the tree, without damaging it, by means of stainless steel cables and textile straps.

NUT
ROOM

❧ The curved shape and limited range of materials create the interior's special effect. Untreated oak, wool felt bed and bench coverings as well as as stainless steel mountings form the surface texture. Various storage spaces, a small heater, and a hi-fi system complement the interior furnishings. Windows on all sides and the vaulted skylight allow plenty of light to enter the room.

TREES - a walnut tree

HEIGHT - terrace: 3.5 m; Nut Room: 4.5 m

STATICS - terrace suspended in the walnut tree by means of steel cables and textile straps; the weight of the treehouse rests on eight asymmetrically arranged, leaning stainless steel supports

TERRACE - glazed oak

INTERIOR AREA - 8.6 sqm

TERRACE AREA - 7.4 sqm

FAÇADE CONSTRUCTION - from inside to outside: 20 mm oak boarding, tongue and groove, untreated; round framework of glazed sheet steel; flanking wooden arch of glued wood; 60 mm mineral insulation; 20 mm spruce boarding; rubber sealed; 20 mm air space; glazed, rounded oak battens

BETWEEN MAGNOLIA AND PINE

MELLE, GERMANY

-

2007

This space is embedded in dense bushes between a magnolia and several pines on a private property at the edge of the Westphalian town of Melle. The clients use it as a retreat and guest room, as well as a playroom for their grandchildren. This arboreal refuge is also an inspiring setting for meetings with business partners or small receptions. The treehouse's design comprises two staggered, square areas at different heights. The terrace area and the closed cube each rest on a precisely crafted framework of brushed stainless steel. Both areas are connected to the stairway by a walkway. Weather-resistant tatajuba wood was used outside on the terrace and the façade. An outdoor shower on the tree-house terrace is refreshing on summer days.

Reddish oak gives the treehouse's elegant interior its distinctive appearance. The sitting and reclining areas on three sides are upholstered in light-grey wool felt with cushions scattered throughout. Beneath these sections, pull-out boxes provide storage space. Other integrated elements, such as a hi-fi system and heater, add the finishing touches to the interior furnishings and ensure that the treehouse is also comfortable in chillier weather. To the south, a large horizontally pivoted sash window offers a spellbinding view as far as the Teutoburg Forest, provided the weather is clear.

TREES	-	one magnolia and some firs
HEIGHT	-	terrace: 3.5 m; treehouse: 4.5 m
STATICS	-	standing framework of brushed stainless steel tube
TERRACE	-	tatajuba
INTERIOR AREA	-	13.6 sqm
TERRACE AREA	-	14.4 sqm
FAÇADE CONSTRUCTION	-	from inside to outside: 20 mm oak boarding, tinted and waxed; 60 mm mineral insulation; wind foil; 20 mm air space; 20 mm tatajuba boarding, horizontal

CLIFF
TREEHOUSE

NEW YORK STATE, USA
-
2007

The client's spectacular private property with its ultra-modern and unusual house is located in the State of New York, two hours north of New York City and close to the Hudson river. The purpose of the first visit was to find a suitable place for the treehouse. There were many possibilities, meaning that no quick decision could be made. Extensive woodland and various clusters of trees were viewed and their pros and cons considered. On the eastern side of the property, there was a steep rock face with a few trees. A spot with a magnificent maple afforded an excellent view of both the house and, further away, of the Hudson. The unique qualities of this location could scarcely be rivalled and triumphed in the end. In line with the client's wishes, the treehouse cabin had to offer enough space for the parents and their two children. The size made it necessary to support the closed construction independently from the tree against the cliff. The loads are distributed across two short steel supports in the upper area and two V-shaped beams beneath the front part of the cabin. Rough-sawn larch planks with a coat of silver paint were used for the treehouse's external boarding. This means that, depending on the light, the surface has a metallic effect and displays a range of different colours.

CLIFF TREEHOUSE

NEW YORK STATE, USA
-
2007

The terrace is made of oak and is fastened to the maple with stainless steel cables and textile straps. To enter the treehouse, one starts at the edge of the cliff, where a narrow, low-gradient ramp leads to the terrace. The visitor can feel the steepness of the slope. The two main branches of the maple run almost exactly through the centre of the oak construction and form the middle of the terrace.

From there, a walkway leads to the cabin, where one is immediately captivated by the breathtaking view of the surrounding landscape.

The generous reclining area is perfect for relaxing and enjoying the distance and altitude. All of the interior surfaces are made of untreated oak and create a peaceful atmosphere. Pull-out boxes and a wide sideboard offer storage space for books and toys. Some of the windows are fixed panes of glass, while others can be opened. The skylight can also be opened, so that visitors can gaze into the tree-tops and, when the weather is fine, enjoy looking at the stars.

TREES	-	a maple tree
HEIGHT	-	1 m to 8 m
STATICS	-	terrace suspended in the maple tree by means of stainless steel cables and textile straps; the treehouse's weight rests on two short steel supports and two v-shaped beams
INTERIOR AREA	-	9.4 sqm
TERRACE AREA	-	10.4 sqm
FAÇADE CONSTRUCTION	-	from inside to outside: oak boarding, tongue and groove, untreated; 19 mm OSB; 80 mm mineral insulation; membrane; 20 mm larch boarding, rough-sawn and painted silver

WORLD OF LIVING

RHEINAU-LINX, GERMANY

—

2008

The company *WeberHaus* in Rheinau-Linx, close to the French border near Strasbourg, is successfully involved in the construction of houses. However, the craftsmen at this longstanding company had never yet built a treehouse. With this ambitious project, the company founder Hans Weber not only wanted to add another attraction to the company-owned construction, residential and adventure park *World of Living*, but also fulfil a personal lifelong dream. Right from the start, the company management was of the view that the new treehouse should be in modern style. All the same, when the design was presented, the clients were surprised since this treehouse was nothing like they had imagined. However, the futuristic shape of the concept managed to convince the innovation-oriented decision-makers at *WeberHaus*. Once the design had met with a positive response, the suitability of two locations within the *World of Living* park was examined. Considerations with regard to park design and the arborist's expertise also went into the assessment, so that finally one of two possible oaks was chosen.

The construction of the treehouse was based on a design from *Baumraum* and undertaken with the expert guidance of a master craftsman and trainer in the company's own apprentice workshop. The treehouse's static system is largely based on two elements: The elliptically-shaped treehouse rests not in the oak itself, but on seven angled and conically-shaped supports made of Siberian larch. The supports are hinged to the treehouse and concrete foundation and stand at different angles to each other. The system used to arrange the supports is not immediately apparent to the observer. During the design phase, a number of framework variants were simulated using models and then optimised with the help of a complex computer system. Unlike the treehouse itself, the loads of the terrace and stairs are braced by the tree. From the terrace, a walkway leads to the higher treehouse. Nor was anything left to chance with regard to the oak's resilience: A tree surveyor examined the oak's health and tested its resilience using modern simulation methods, ensuring that the treehouse stands firmly and safely, even during severe storms.

The vaulted interior welcomes visitors with scenic wallpaper which shows the crown of the oak as it would be seen without the treehouse. The photography also contains text blocks in German, English, and French, which associatively describe the tree as a special living organism in all its diversity. Even after spending a great deal of time in the treehouse, one can still discover new plays on words hidden amongst the leaves. The interior is in indigenous oak and its solid finishing means it can also handle large numbers of visitors. The roll containers and pull-out boxes integrated into the seating areas can be used either as meeting tables or for storage.

TREES	- an oak
HEIGHT	- terrace: 5 m; cabin: 6.5 m
STATICS	- terrace suspended from the oak by means of stainless steel cables and textile straps; the treehouse's weight rests on seven asymmetrically arranged, and conically-shaped supports made of larch (glued wood)
BEARING STRUCTURE	- untreated larch
TERRACE	- 32.6 sqm
INTERIOR AREA	- 8.8 sqm
FAÇADE CONSTRUCTION	- from inside to outside: picture wallpaper; 11 mm plasterboard; 20 mm larch boarding; steel framework (laser parts); flanking wooden arch of larch with 100 mm mineral insulation; 20 mm spruce boarding; foil; 20 mm battens/air space; lasered larch boarding, rounded
ROOFING	- sheet zinc, preoxidised as standing seam roofing

TREEHOUSE BACHSTELZE

EBERSCHWANG, AUSTRIA

-

2008

❧ Eberschwang is a small community in the Austrian district of Ried im Innkreis, between the cities of Salzburg and Linz. Despite its beautiful landscape, this rural region does not belong to the country's best-known tourist destinations. Nor in terms of contemporary architecture does this area lay any claim to being a site of pilgrimage for architects as is the case, say, for Vorarlberg. Naturally, this does not mean that the inhabitants of Ried im Innkreis do not have an eye for modern architecture or appreciate it in their midst. The client's family likes to spend holidays and weekends at its second home, enjoying the quality of country life and getting together with relatives. Although the children are still very young, they already appreciate the benefits of a treehouse. The adults do in any case. The clients wanted the treehouse to be built beside a small stream on the southern edge of their property. It was also important to them that one could see the main house and the landscape from the treehouse and vice versa. The architecture of the treehouse did not necessarily have to correspond with the usual visual standards – experimentation with regard to shape and material was permitted. Another highly appealing idea was that of being able to catch trout from the treehouse terrace. Following a number of sketches, a design was developed with a very long, narrow terrace with a separate treehouse.

TREEHOUSE BACHSTELZE

The oxidised corten steel lends the treehouse cabin, with its sloping surfaces, a very sculptural appearance. The reddish glaze of the treehouse terrace and the support structure has been co-ordinated to match the metal's rusty surface. Angular windows afford a view in all directions and their shape is subordinated into the overall look. The terrace is largely anchored in the trees, while the treehouse's weight rests on eight asymmetrical, slanting oak stilts. The two elements are connected by means of a small walkway with stairs.

Inside the treehouse cabin the visitor is met by surfaces made of untreated oak. The built-in furnishings include upholstered reclining and sitting areas, integrated pull-out drawers and a sideboard. At the end of the treehouse, the large panorama window offers a fantastic view of the trees and meadows. A special feature here is the horizontal glassed area which adjoins this window almost seamlessly and overlooks the little stream below. An integrated hi-fi system with powerful speakers is good enough for even the most demanding music lover. Whether there is electro music or birdsong to be heard in the background, this long-legged refuge is definitely a space which appeals to all senses.

TREES	-	one birch and two ashs
HEIGHT	-	terrace: 3.5 m; cabin: 4.6 m
STATICS	-	terrace suspended in a birch and two ash trees; two beams support the front part of the terrace; the treehouse's weight rests on eight asymmetrically arranged, sloped oak stilts
TERRACE	-	oak, glazed
INTERIOR AREA	-	8.8 sqm
TERRACE AREA	-	13.6 sqm
FAÇADE CONSTRUCTION	-	from inside to outside: oak boarding, tongue and groove, untreated; 19 mm OSB; 80 mm mineral insulation; membrane; 20 mm air space; 4 mm corten steel sheet, oxidised

TREEHOUSE DJUREN

GROSS IPPENER, GERMANY
-
2008

Compared with *Baumraum* projects in Italy or overseas, this construction was quite an easy task in logistical terms. The site in Lower Saxony is very near Bremen and is also very close to the assembly location. Thus, one can almost describe it as home territory. However, the shape of the treehouse and the associated details offered enough challenges to the designers and the craftsmen building it. The property is on the edge of the village with a few detached houses and plenty of trees. The clients wanted an unusual and comfortable treehouse – a nest for the whole family. How this wish was to be implemented was left entirely to *Baumraum*. The rounded shape of this treehouse is reminiscent of an egg cut open longitudinally. This association is heightened through the accentuation of the gable surfaces with cream-painted perspex and the elliptically-shaped windows. On the other hand, the materials chosen for the other external elements, such as the terrace and the underside of the treehouse, are more robust since these are made of indigenous oak. Sheet zinc was used for the treehouse roof. One special feature is the curved glass area on the front façade. The weight of the treehouse is borne by both the trees and by supports. The weight of the two terraces and the horizontal load of the treehouse is distributed across the oaks by means of steel cables and textile straps.

TREEHOUSE DJUREN

❦ The interior's special features are the curved shape and limited materials used. White painted surfaces, plenty of windows and the curved sitting and reclining areas covered in grey wool felt lend this space an ethereal character. The emphasis is placed on the oiled oak used in the flooring and the window frames. The pull-out box fronts are made of perspex with inlaid reddish bamboo.

TREES	– two oaks
HEIGHT	– lower terrace: 3.8 m; upper terrace and treehouse: 5.6 m
STATICS	– the weight of the terraces and the horizontal loads of the treehouse are distributed across the two oaks by means of steel cables and textile straps; the vertical loads rest on four v-shaped steel supports
TERRACE	– untreated oaks
INTERIOR AREA	– 10.6 sqm
TERRACE AREA	– 16.4 sqm
FAÇADE CONSTRUCTION	– from inside to outside: 8 mm latex painted plasterboard; steel framework with flanking wooden arch of glued wood; 80 mm mineral insulation; 20 mm spruce boarding; membrane; 20 mm air space; rounded oak boarding; gable areas: perspex, 8 mm painted cream on reverse side
ROOFING	– sheet zinc

CAPOREA
BIRCH
PAVILION

PITTI BIMBO WINTER FAIR, FLORENCE, ITALY
-
JANUARY 2008

Presentation of the pavilion at the World Congress of Architecture on the campus of the Castello del Valentino in Italy.

🌳 Twice a year children's fashion manufacturers present their latest creations at the Pitti Bimbo trade fair in Florence. Dealers and specialist press meet at the Fortezza da Basso exhibition grounds to be presented with an overview of the latest collections at the industry's most important trade fair. CAPOREA, a young Italian fashion design label, specialises in children's clothing and commissioned *Baumraum* to build its pavilion. The company's management was fascinated by the idea of presenting its products in a treehouse. The implemented concept was a free interpretation of the 'treehouse' theme and focused on creating an emblematic and sculptural effect. The design is based on the use of birches.

WINDING NEST

TRIENNALE DI MILANO, ITALY

–

2008

The *Triennale di Milano Design Museum* is one of Italy's most respected museums of contemporary architecture and design. The museum's *Casa per tutti* exhibition was entirely dedicated to the subject of 'living'. The curators chose to show experimental approaches, utopias, and applied concepts from past decades and the present. Alongside other architecture offices presented at the exhibition, *Baumraum* was asked to create a temporary spatial sculpture in the museum park. The installation comprises countless larch batons which spiral around the trunk of a great lime tree. The spatial sculpture starts from the ground with only a few batons, winds around the trunk and solidifies at the top into a nest.

FROG
PRINCE

MÜNSTER, GERMANY

-

2009

The clients wanted a small haven where they could read and relax in their own garden, but the existing fruit trees on the property were too small to support a treehouse. However, the garden did contain a small pond that was almost completely dry. Rotten timbers framed the edge of what had once been home to ornamental goldfish. Our clients were very taken with the idea of refurbishing the old pond and setting their garden hideaway high above the surface of the water. Water lilies float around three slabs of natural stone that lead to the accessway in the middle of the pond. The high-grade terrace made of tatajuba planking rests on a stainless steel frame and offers space for a small sun deck. From there, a few steps and a narrow walkway provide access to the raised cocoon. The underside of the rounded structure above the pond is covered with zinc sheeting and narrow lamellae made of tatajuba wood. Resting on eight asymmetrically arranged stainless steel supports, it features large, rounded glass surfaces at the gables as well as two long, narrow windows in its side walls that illuminate the interior and give the structure a light, transparent appearance.

FROG
PRINCE

MÜNSTER, GERMANY
-
2009

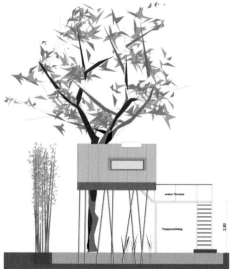

Inside the cabin, the first thing that catches the eye is the large, convex skylight that extends almost all the way over the reclining platform. Large drawers under the opposite bed and bench areas provide storage space. The walls, floor, and furniture are made of ash wood and varnished white to underscore the sophisticated yet restrained character of the design. A few months after the construction work was complete, amphibians began to move into the pond. Today, the cabin can serve as a vantage point on spring and summer evenings from which to watch the frogs and listen to their croaking in the water below.

TREES	between fruit trees
HEIGHT	lower terrace: 2.8 m; catwalk and cabin: 4 m
STATICS	the weight of the cabin is supported by 8 asymmetrically arranged stainless steel supports; the terrace rests on four stainless steel supports
TERRACE	stainless steel frame with tatajuba planking
INTERIOR AREA	8.6 sqm
TERRACE AREA	9.0 sqm
FAÇADE STRUCTURE	from inside to outside: 20 mm ash slats, varnished white; round ribs of steel flanked with laminated wooden arches; 60 mm insulation; 20 mm spruce boarding; sand layer; 20 mm zinc sheeting, underside: lamellae made of curved tatajuba slats
ROOFING	zinc sheeting

BÂLVEDERE TREEHOUSE

BASEL, SWITZERLAND
-
2009

The clients wanted a vantage point on their property that would afford a view of the city of Basel and the faraway Vosges mountains. To fulfil their wish, the treehouse had to be constructed at a considerable height in a clump of four spruce trees. As the trees had grown at an angle, the greatest challenge was finding a geometry for the access to the treehouse. Additionally, strong vibrations induced by wind and storms had to be taken into account. Three ladders and two intermediate landings provide access to the upper terrace and treehouse cabin, which stands at a height of twelve metres above ground. The cabin offers a breathtaking view of the city of Basel through the branches of a large spruce tree. On a clear day, one can see all the way to France. Copper was chosen for the façade of the rectangular treehouse. The metal will gradually lose its brilliant shine and will then blend almost invisibly into its surroundings.

BÂLVEDERE TREEHOUSE

BASEL, SWITZERLAND
–
2009

The use of oiled oak on the inner surfaces and the grey wool felt of the couch upholstery create a warm and friendly atmosphere in this little room in the treetops. There are windows on each wall as well as a large skylight to provide a view in all directions. The three levels and the access ladders are illuminated after dark by outdoor lamps.

TREES	four spruce trees
HEIGHT	first level: 4 m; second level: 8 m; third level: 12 m
STATICS	suspended from the spruce trees using stainless steel tree screws and webbing belts
TERRACE	untreated larch wood
INTERIOR AREA	6.2 sqm
TERRACE AREA	18.4 sqm
FAÇADE STRUCTURE	from inside to outside: 20 mm oiled oak boarding; 20 mm plywood; 60 mm insulation; wind foil; 20 mm ventilation; 20 mm plywood; irregularly arranged copper panels

TREEHOUSE
PRAGUE

NEAR PRAGUE, THE CZECH REPUBLIC

-

2010

This treehouse is located in a forested area in direct proximity to the client's residence near the Czech capital. A preliminary inspection of the site with the clients and their two children revealed a number of feasible locations for a treehouse. The tree that was initially selected was a large robinia. More detailed examination, however, revealed that the tree was damaged. Therefore, the treehouse was finally constructed in a sturdy oak tree. It consists of two terraces on two levels, at a height of 3.5 and 4.5 metres respectively, and a square treehouse cabin. The terrace structure and the front part of the cabin body are suspended from the oak tree by a system of ropes and belt loops. Two cylindrical steel supports at the rear of the treehouse prevent excessive stress on the tree.

TREEHOUSE PRAGUE

NEAR PRAGUE, THE CZECH REPUBLIC
-
2010

🐛 Untreated larch wood was chosen for the façade of the treehouse cube and the terraces, while the interior was executed in oiled oak. Identical, spacious windows on three sides of the treehouse combine with a large skylight to allow light to flood the interior and offer a view of the surrounding trees on all sides.

TREES	one oak tree
HEIGHT	first level: 3.5 m; second level: 4.5 m
STATICS	suspension by means of steel cables and webbing belts from the oak tree, two cylindrical columns at the rear of the tree house
TERRACE	untreated larch wood
INTERIOR AREA	7 sqm
TERRACE AREA	lower terrace: 13 sqm; upper terrace: 7 sqm
FAÇADE STRUCTURE	from inside to outside: 20 mm oiled oak boarding; 60 mm insulation; wind foil; 20 mm ventilation; 22 mm larch boarding, installed horizontally and vertically at the corners

COPPER CUBE

WERDER NEAR BERLIN, GERMANY

–

2010

The Copper Cube is a gem of a treehouse that features an integrated bathroom and offers all the comfort of a fully-fledged residence. Its unique location, offering a view of the Großer Zernsee lake near Potsdam, makes this treehouse a particularly attractive weekend retreat for its owners. The treehouse consists of a terrace at a height of four metres above ground and a square treehouse cabin at a height of five metres. While the body of the treehouse rests on an independent steel structure, the large terrace is suspended by cables from an oak tree. Copper panels were chosen for the façade. The metal was coated with ultraflexible clear lacquer to protect it from oxidation and preserve the reddish colour of the copper. The Copper Cube shows that even a treehouse can be habitable throughout the year and that it can offer every modern convenience.

The interior of this treehouse features large beds and sofas, a desk, wardrobe, and minibar as well as electricity and heat. The dominant material of the interior design is oiled oak panelling. As a special feature, there is an integrated bathroom with a shower, toilet and sink. The water and electricity supply lines are hidden in one of the columns.

TREES	-	one oak tree
HEIGHT	-	first level: 4 m; second level: 5 m
STATICS	-	the treehouse cabin rests on four steel columns; the terrace structure and the front section of the treehouse body are suspended from the oak tree by a system of cables and belt loops
TERRACE	-	varnished larch
INTERIOR AREA	-	17 sqm
TERRACE AREA	-	18.4 sqm
ACCOUTREMENTS	-	beds and couches; desk; minibar; wardrobe; bathroom with shower and toilet
FAÇADE STRUCTURE	-	from inside to outside: 20 mm oiled oak boarding; 20 mm plywood; 100 mm insulation; wind foil; 20 mm ventilation; 20 mm plywood; copper panels with oxidation-proof finish

SOLLING TREEHOUSE

SCHÖNHAGEN NEAR USLAR, GERMANY

-

2010

The site of this treehouse near the town of Uslar in Lower Saxony is located beside an old forester's house in a small side valley. Access to the property is provided by a forest road that winds along a small brook with a few ponds. The house was restored with great effort and dedication, while its surroundings were carefully landscaped. Natural stone walls, newly planted indigenous trees and two large artificial pond habitats have turned the place into a sanctuary for nature lovers and a haven for flora and fauna alike. Thus, the site is in many ways the perfect location for a treehouse.

The clients wanted a treehouse that would provide joy to their young son and friends of the family for many years to come.

SOLLING TREEHOUSE

SCHÖNHAGEN NEAR USLAR, GERMANY
-
2010

A handsome stand of hemlock spruce by the lower of the two ponds was chosen as the site of the treehouse. Soon the decision was made to set a two-storey treehouse tower into the pond itself and connect it with the hemlock spruces by means of a long terrace. The stairs, which form the access to the treehouse terrace, are located at the water's edge. Two of the trees pierce the terrace to welcome visitors to the treehouse. From this vantage point, the narrow deck of larch wood seems to float above the water of the pond until it reaches the curved treehouse tower. Here the visitor can choose to enter the room on the lower level or to take another exterior stairway to reach the upper sleeping area. Both levels are equipped with plenty of loungers and benches as well as storage space and electrical connections. During the day, the treehouse serves as a vantage point for observing creatures in the water and the adjoining meadows. Fish, frogs and even deer can be sighted from here. At night, the upper room is a comfortable place to sleep and dream and – when the skies are clear – to gaze at the stars through the domed skylight.

TREES	- hemlock spruces
HEIGHT	- lower terrace: 4.2 m above the pond surface; upper terrace: 2.6 m higher
STATICS	- the weight of the treehouse tower is supported by 12 slanting stainless steel supports; the terrace is suspended from several hemlock spruces by means of steel cables and webbing belts
TERRACE	- larch wood (laminated beams as girders); stainless steel railings with woven netting
INTERIOR AREA	- 11 sqm
TERRACE AREA	- 26 sqm
FAÇADE STRUCTURE	- from inside to outside: 20 mm larch boarding; 20 mm spruce boarding; round ribs of steel flanked with laminated wooden arches; 100 mm insulation; 20 mm spruce boarding; sand layer; lamellae of rounded larch slats
ROOFING	- zinc sheeting

TREEHOUSE ON THE SPREE

BERLIN, GERMANY
-

2011

One of Berlin's many unique features is its un-developed areas in the eastern parts of Berlin – just at the edge of the city centre. The particular charm of many of these areas lies in the old commercial buildings amid huge expanses of urban wilderness. Though completely neglected for years, more and more of this urban wasteland has recently become the location for alternative activities, suburban leisure and recreational activities, and new urban development projects. Particularly along the banks of the Spree, restaurants, cafés, and a whole range of leisure attractions have been created. This project was conceived by a developer who saw the potential of a river location for his business and a marina at one of the old river ports. The port has meanwhile been redeveloped and several yachts, boathouses and a floating hostel are moored here. A magnificent weeping willow situated directly on the edge of the embankment inspired him to build a treehouse.

TREEHOUSE ON THE SPREE

BERLIN, GERMANY
-
2011

The result is a rounded, metallic tree cabin direct on the bank of the Spree. The construction is anchored by a combination of supports and cables connected to the willow, thus spreading the load of the rear of the cabin and stabilising the cabin's horizontal position. The outer shell of the cabin is clad with three metres of stainless steel sheeting, which was cut using digital laser technology. The interior is furnished with a bedding area for two to three people, sofa and a folding table or workspace. The white walls and ceiling, as well as the high-gloss coated fitted furniture, lends the cabin a light and elegant atmosphere. The flooring and the furniture edging are finished with oak.

The large windows offer a splendid view of the water, passing boats and maritime activities in the small port facility.

TREES - weeping willow

HEIGHT - between 2.5 and 5.0 m

STATICS - the weight of the cabin rests on five slanting steel supports, the rear part of the treehouse is held by steel suspension cables and textile straps

INTERIOR AREA - 8.4 sqm

FAÇADE STRUCTURE - from inside to outside: 8 mm plasterboard painted with latex; steel framework flanked with wooden arch of glued wood; 60 mm mineral insulation; 20 mm spruce boarding; membrane; 20 mm air space; 3 mm stainless steel sheets; rounded part: zinc sheeting

ROOFING - rubber

THE TREEHOUSE

HECHTEL-EKSEL, BELGIUM

-

2012

The international paper company Sappi and its communication agency Proximity BBDO wanted to underline their commitment to sustainability and environmental protection by constructing a treehouse. In the search for new partners and a suitable location for this ambitious project, the Belgian municipality of Hechtel-Eksel and the Flemish Agency for Nature and Forests were recommended as partners. The treehouse was to be a place where project partners and external groups could assemble and discuss topics such as sustainability and environmental protection.

The goal was to create a location that inspires people and helps them to confront important issues outside their daily business routine. *Baumraum* was commissioned with the design of this special treehouse. A clearing with several beautiful pine trees was selected as a building site. The fundamental idea for the design of the treehouse is based on folding a sheet of paper, which seamlessly connects the interior and exterior.
'The Treehouse' consists of five elements: two cabins at different levels, connecting terraces, flights of stairs and the connecting roof element.

THE
TREEHOUSE

HECHTEL-EKSEL, BELGIUM
-
2012

The cabins and upper terraces rest on 19 slanting steel supports in free arrangement, while the lower staircase and intermediate landing are suspended from the pine tree by means of steel cables and textile belts. The steel supports are fastened to the ground with drilling screws. Due to this technique it is possible to dispense with the use of concrete and minimise interference with the forest floor. The lower floor accommodates a café lounge, a small pantry, a bathroom and the utility room.

THE
TREEHOUSE

HECHTEL-EKSEL, BELGIUM
–
2012

The centrepiece of the treehouse is the upper level – the exquisite conference room among the trees. Softly upholstered benches on three sides emphasise the relaxed ambience of the room and are pleasantly comfortable. The elegant interior on both levels was further accentuated by scenic wallpaper that depicts branches on the straight and rounded ceilings. Using chalk, visitors can give free reign to their creative ideas on the bathroom walls coated with blackboard paint. State-of-the-art technology by the company Jaga

was used for the heating and air conditioning. A heat pump, which is located underground, extracts heat from the ambient air and transfers it via a steel support and piping system into the treehouse by means of a liquid medium. The result of this technology is carbon neutral and thus creates comfortable indoor climatic conditions at low energy costs. The system also allows the rooms to be cooled in summer. The lighting of the treehouse is achieved through LED technology with minimum energy consumption.

Visit www.the-treehouse.be
for further information

TREES	-	between pine trees in a clearing
HEIGHT	-	lower level 5.50 m; upper level 6.50 m
STATICS	-	the cabins and upper terraces rest on 19 slanting steel supports in free arrangement. The lower terraces and intermediate terrace are suspended from a pine tree by means of steel cables and textile belts
STRUCTURE	-	untreated larch wood
TERRACE	-	20.4 sqm
TERRACE CONSTRUCTION	-	steel frame with larch boarding
INTERIOR AREA	-	lower level 24.0 sqm, upper level 26 sqm
FAÇADE CONSTRUCTION	-	from inside to outside: 12 mm gypsum, vapour barrier, 100 mm natural insulating material; 100 mm five-layer solid wood panels; sarking felt; 20 mm air space; horizontal larch boarding
ROOF CURVATURE AND ROOF EDGES	-	preweathered zinc metal sheet
LIGHTING	-	Nimbus LED lights MODUL Q 49 LED, MODUL Q 49 AQUA LED (outside), MODUL Q 36 IQ MASTER LED

AROUND THE OAK

HALLE (WESTFALEN), GERMANY
-

2014

In an ordinary house, the distance from the ground is perceived to be less challenging and suspenseful. One feels confined to the earth and perhaps safer. In a tall treehouse like this, everything is different. Here, one feels transported from the ground, caught somewhere between heaven and earth – a high altitude experience that triggers special feelings. The ascent to the top increases the anticipation and opens the door to linger in the complex and living organism tree. Ths treehouse in Halle/Westfalen is situated at a considerable height of more than eleven metres above the ground. Even the accession is by no means routine. First, one enters an old barn and then steps into the open air via a steep set of stairs and a trapdoor in the roof. From there, one continues across a small walkway to the actual entrance. A spiral staircase made of stainless steel coils around the oak. When negotiating the staircase, the ascent to the treehouse becomes a memorable experience. One remains within touching distance to the oak, encircling its trunk below and above forked branches, twisting upwards to the access hatch of the treehouse terrace, so to speak.

This terrace, which was made of tatajuba timber boards, offers space for a table and a few chairs. Here, one has a dreamlike view of the surrounding fields and a few residential buildings in the vicinity. The exterior of the circular treehouse cabin is clad in zinc sheet metal roofing and narrow larch slats at the face ends. In the cabin, the visitor's glance falls first on the arched roof window above the lie down area. Large circular glass surfaces on the gable sides and two long narrow windows on the long sides illuminate the interior and offer multiple views of the crown of the oak. The interior design, as well as the walls and floor, are made of white varnished ash and thus emphasise the sophisticated and understated character of the design. However, in order to enjoy the sensuous experience and comfort of this treehouse, a few regulatory obstacles had to first be circumnavigated.

In many cases, obtaining a building permit for a treehouse is not a major hurdle. However, in the implementation of this project the path towards acquiring a legal basis for the developers and for us proved to be very rocky.

The fact that parts of the treehouse were to be built above a small public road presented the local authorities with considerable challenges. Following extensive correspondence and visits by the urban administration, a proper solution for both parties was finally agreed upon. The compromise stipulated that, contrary to the original plan, the terrace of the treehouse would be scaled down so that public land would not be built upon. A few particular safety requirements by the building authorities were also to be met.

AROUND
THE OAK

HALLE (WESTFALEN), GERMANY
-
2014

❦ The ambitious plans could only be examined in more detail once the design had finally been given the green light. The towering height, as well as the accession from the barn and spiral staircase, were a challenge for the planners and companies commissioned.

After the oak had been measured by a 3D scanner with regard to the key points, the geometry of the spiral staircase could be designed and perfectly implemented by the metal processing plant of Andreas Meschter. The terrace and cabin were assembled using tree climbers, a lifting platform and mobile crane, which was deployed for a short period of time. The idea of suspending the entire structure from the oak by means of steel cables, textile belts and two slanting supports was also an ambitious task which eventually proved successful. The fact that this treehouse became reality after more than two years is due to the tenacity and special passion of our clients Gerlinde and Horst.

We are delighted with the treehouse and hope that our clients have many pleasant hours in their never-never land at a height of eleven metres.

TREES	- an oak
HEIGHT	- upper terrace and cabin: 11.20 m
STATICS	- the weight of the spiral staircase, terrace and treehouse cabin is distributed across the oak by means of steel cables and textile belts. Two slanting stainless steel supports transmit the external loads of the cabin to the trunk of the oak at a low height
TERRACE	- 9.0 sqm
TERRACE CONSTRUCTION	- larch beams (laminated beams) tatajuba timber boards (FSC certified)
INTERIOR AREA	- 8.6 sqm
CABIN CONSTRUCTION	- from inside to outside: 20 mm ash boarding, white varnished; round ribs of steel flanked with laminated wooden arches; 60 mm insulation; 20 mm spruce boarding; sand layer; 20 mm curved larch slats
ROOFING	- zinc sheeting

TREEHOUSES
IN OLDENBURG
CASTLE GARDEN

OLDENBURG, GERMANY
-
2014

In 2014 a notable event for Oldenburg Castle Garden took place. This beautiful park had been created 200 years earlier and has since become a sanctuary for botanists and those looking for a place to relax in the city centre. The anniversary was celebrated with various events and exhibitions. The organisers had the idea of building one or more treehouses, thus enabling an appreciation of the park and the particularly beautiful trees for a limited time.

Our concept included five identical cubes which were to be installed in prime locations in the park. Four of these 2.5 by 2.5 metre large compartments were to hover among groups of trees.

One of the cubes was to be situated in the castle pond and reached via a walkway at the bank of the pond. Following an efficient installation, the treehouses were inaugurated on 25 April 2014 at an anniversary event in the presence of Stephan Weil, the Prime Minister of Lower Saxony, and made available to the public.

Visitors could now have a picnic among the leaves and view the park from a different perspective. The treehouses added a nice touch: from there, visitors could glance over a high wall at the part of the park that was not accessible to the public and thus witness at close proximity the beautiful blossoms of the tulip trees.

OLDENBURG CASTLE GARDEN

OLDENBURG, GERMANY
-
2014

❦ The colour concept of the capsules, which are fitted with acrylic glass, was intended to underline the unique character of each setting. Thus, the white treehouse in the tulip trees corresponds to the colour of the blossoms, while the dark blue treehouse by the kitchen garden wall reflects the enchanted look of the place. A group of primeval redwood trees were assigned a black cube, whereas a striking light-blue treehouse at the park entrance near a large meadow hovers between two stately tree and welcomes visitors. The treehouse above the surface of the castle pond acquired the colour of magenta, in conformity with the blossoms of the water lilies. The treehouses, which are equipped with benches and a table, invite one to linger for a short or long period of time.

During their existence of four and a half months, the spatial installations were very popular places for people of all ages. Each treehouse was equipped with guestbooks which rapidly filled with entries. Some – young visitors in most cases – furnished these places with small inscriptions and engravings on the benches and tables. This kind of appropriation was not part of the concept and at first was met with little enthusiasm by the park administration. After a while, however, one learnt to appreciate this form of lively communication and individual expression.

The inauguration of the treehouses by Lower Saxony's Prime Minister Stephan Weil

TREES	- two tulip trees; a primeval redwood tree and a cedar; two oaks; two primeval redwood trees
HEIGHT	- 3.20 m
STATICS	- four treehouses are suspended from two trees by means of steel cables and textile belts; the treehouse at the castle pond rests on a frame made of steel rods and large steel legs in the water
INTERIOR AREA	- 6 sqm
CABIN CONSTRUCTION	- floor: steel frame with larch boarding; walls: framework of larch timber beams 80 x 80 mm; 21 mm wire mesh plywood; 6 mm acrylic colour-coated on the rear side

OBSERVATION TOWER AT THE MARSHY WOODLAND IN BOLLENHAGEN

JADE, NORDMENTZHAUSEN, GERMANY

-

2014

☙ The marshy woodland in Bollenhagen is situated in a former wetland of the municipality of Jade. Since 2008, a new setting of oaks, birches and willows has emerged around a 150-year old mixed oak forest. Bulrush swamps, extensively used grasslands and a lake are also located here. The exploration station 'Bollwerk' is located in the eastern part of the project area and provides details on the recultivation project. Here one can also practise recognising the chirping of birds. The idea arose to experience the development of the woodland and marshy areas from a treehouse. Following various studies and designs, the concept of the 'observation tower' emerged, with particular emphasis on being able to experience the trees. Exploring with an elevating platform was of enormous benefit during the decision-making process. The tower was to provide a covered viewing platform and particularly include the surrounding oaks.

In relation to the legislation on construction, building a structure in a natural landscape is not an easy affair. From a legal perspective, the 'undeveloped outskirt area' must be kept clear of buildings – unless, for example, there is public interest and environmentally important aspects speak in favour of the proposal. In most cases, financing issues are not clarified in a couple of weeks – particularly in the case of a public project – and patience is required before the necessary funds from various household coffers can be secured. It is fortunate that the client-representative of the district of Wesermarsch has great skill and determination, as well as a distinct feeling for modern architecture. Together we presented the project to the community and funding bodies during a number of meetings.

After a few setbacks, but with a positive final outcome, the project 'observation tower' could be implemented after more than two years of preparation.

MARSHY WOODLAND IN BOLLENHAGEN

JADE, NORDMENTZHAUSEN, GERMANY
-
2014

In accordance with the guidelines, construction work was tendered out. This task in itself is a complex undertaking. However, it went very quickly once the construction firms were finally established. In a short time, a construction road was paved and eight 'displacement piles' – each with a length of ten metres – were driven into the moorland. The steel structure of the tower was then speedily assembled on the concrete panel above the ground. A carpentry firm undertook the cladding of the tower in larch timber beams, as well as the necessary roofing work.

The use of the tower is possible via uniformly arranged steps which lead to the visitor platforms. Visitors can experience the surrounding crowns of oaks and scenery from different angles on four platforms at differing heights. A special feature is the five-metre long walkway, in which one can almost walk into the foliage of the trees. The sheltered visitor platform invites most visitors to linger for a long period. However, in typical Northern German weather conditions one can only tolerate this for a while in order to permit one's gaze to roam over the scenery.

TREES	-	in a group of oaks
HEIGHT	-	level 1: 5.30 m, level 2: 6.50 m, level 3 (covered): 9.00 m, level 4 : 11.50 m: overall height: 12.80 m
STATICS	-	steel frame with closed sections; deep foundation with 8 displacement piles beneath a slab of reinforced concrete
FAÇADE	-	freshly sawn larch timber beams (FSC certified) 50 x 50 mm at a distance of approx. 45 mm
ROOFING	-	grating tread; double-layer bitumen liner on a slope on larch boarding

CASA EMILIO

ORVIETO, ITALY
-
2015

A few years earlier, our clients from Munich had purchased a dilapidated country house with a large plot of land near the medieval town of Orvieto in the Italian province of Umbria. With great effort and much love, the spacious main house and the smaller outbuildings were renovated and tastefully furnished. A pool was also built at the highest point of the property and many special places to linger were created.

A real treasure of the property is the stock of old oak trees. The mightiest of them is certainly more than 350 years old. With its gigantic crown the tree forms the central shady place on the property.

The idea of adding a treehouse to the ensemble was not only a good fit for the tree population, but also for the desire to create a special retreat and an additional sleeping place for the family and their guests.

The planning for this treehouse succeeded even though we did not visit the property beforehand. The client and I discussed our proposals through some very pleasant, humorous phone and email exchanges, and ultimately we arrived at an agreement.All components were prepared in the workshops in Northern Germany and brought to Italy by truck. After two complex assemblies at the Starnberger lake in Bavaria, our team of five drove further south to Umbria to erect the treehouse at its destination.

With the team accommodated in the dreamlike dwelling house, the conditions for the assembly time were extremely pleasant. An Italian construction company around the ever-helpful Fabrizio supported us on site with the crane assembly as well as with the logistics. The beautiful late summer weather was interrupted by rain and strong winds only once, but this made our tight assembly workload slightly tighter than planned. In the end, however, we managed to complete the treehouse by the time the client arrived. On this sunny day, I met our client Emilio in person for the first time. We discussed the remaining plumbing work for the toilet, the electrical installations and the additional fixtures with the Italian craftsmen, who were then to complete the work without us.

Already during the assembly I enjoyed the place very much. So I could not refuse Emilio's extremely generous offer to enjoy this heavenly spot with my family. Already we've spent portions of several vacations at the property with our children and our friends, taking in the landscape and the many locations to explore and play in – as well as enjoying the large oak trees and the treehouse.

Mille grazie Emilio!

🐓 The rustically furnished interior is lined on all sides with larch and equipped with a double bed, a retractable desk and a toilet. Here, too, the signature of the client is reflected by means of lovingly selected objects. The rooster is the coat of arms of the house. That is why it adorns the walls as well as numerous other places throughout the treehouse and forms the signature which can be found even in the most hidden places on the property.

Through the large windows you look out onto the mighty oak tree that permeates the terrace. Here you are surrounded by treetops, and on a hot afternoon you can lie in the hammock, protected by the shade from the leaves, and maybe read a little or take a nap.

TREES	-	one oak
HEIGHT	-	3.40 m to 4.50 m
STATICS	-	the loads of the terrace and the front part of the treehouse are carried by an oak tree via steel cables and textile belts: two steel columns carry the larger part of the loads in the rear part of the treehouse
TERRACE COVERING	-	larch untreated
INTERIOR AREA	-	10.0 sqm
TERRACE AREA	-	14.4 sqm
FAÇADE STRUCTURE	-	from the inside to the outside: 20 mm larch boarding; 21 mm OSB: 100 mm insulation; underlayment; 30 mm rear ventilation; 22 mm larch floor-ceiling boarding glazed black.

POND HOUSE

OSNABRÜCK, GERMANY

–

2016

When you hear the word 'pond house' you tend to think of a small, dark wooden angler's hut, a shed in which fishing rods, nets and old garden tools are stored.

This small piece of architecture, which hovers above a garden pond near Osnabrück, does not quite fit into this image. This dynamically shaped space above the water makes the viewer think more of a walk-in art sculpture.

The pond house with its skilfully crafted, bronze-tinted stainless steel façade rests on a slanted, gray concrete foundation. The slightly curved surfaces of the mirrored stainless steel sheets slightly distort the surroundings, interacting with the light, and playing color and reflection games with the water, the sky and the surrounding plants.

The interior, made entirely of oak, is rather minimalist, equipped only with a large reclining surface, a sideboard and a small table. However, the pond house serves not only as an ornament in the garden; it is a place to dream and spend the night. Here the builder could, for example, read to his grandchildren from *Little Aquarius* by Otfried Preußler. With a little luck, the grandfather and his grandchildren can then watch the relatives of Cyprinus, the carp, through the horizontal glass surface at the end of the bed. At night, on the other hand, when the sky is clear, you can look up at the starry sky through the slanted skylight and listen to the frogs croaking.

STUCTURE - foundation on reinforced concrete block, cabin: wooden frame construction reinforced with steel elements.

INTERIOR SURFACE - 8 sqm

FAÇADE STRUCTURE - from inside to outside: solid oak oiled, 22 mm OSB, wood frame construction with 100 insulation; underlay; ventilation level; 22 mm OSB; RIMEX SuperMirror Bronze

TREEHOUSE WACHE 6

ATRIUM OF THE CENTRAL LIBRARY BREMEN, GERMANY

-

2016

'Wache 6', the name given to the historically-styled house in the heart of Bremen, testifies to its old use as a police and court building. Through an extensive reconstruction several years ago, the house was extensively rebuilt and put to a new use.

The city library and other tenants became new users of the building and it developed into a crowd-puller in the Hanseatic city.

However, the central foyer of the city library suffered from a lack of quality experiences to attract and hold visitors. So the owners of the property decided to give the atrium a new attractive face and opened it up to include various gastronomical experiences. One component of the new design concept was a space-within-a-space at a central location within the atrium.

The purpose of the space-within-a-space was to structure the atrium and provide a special accent.

All those involved in the planning, including the clients, quickly decided that the term 'treehouse' should be associated with the project. This is how we came into play.

Without a doubt, this task at this prominent location represented a very attractive challenge for us as planners. The task was to plan a spatial sculpture that would fit into the atrium and interpret the association of a treehouse even without existing trees.

Our design featured a floating spatial body with a glass façade and a white steel structure in the front area of the atrium. The four glass façades, the floor and the ceiling surfaces were to be printed with graphic tree branches.

Seven irregularly spaced columns support the body of the space, and two additional columns support the two-flight staircase, with a tapered stair landing at mid-height.

After our design had passed through the diverse committees and ultimately received broad support, the partly complex technical issues of the project had to be solved.

The load transfer to the underground parking garage below and the integration of the assembly process into the ongoing operation of the building were particular technical challenges.

After a quick assembly of the stilt house, the floor coverings and the fixed fixtures were installed and the plantings were arranged. Despite considerable time pressure, the furnishings for the new catering facilities were still being created, so that the newly designed atrium of Station 6 could be inaugurated and made available to the public on schedule. Somewhat later, the furnishing of the 'treehouse' was also carried out by the affiliated Japanese restaurant 'ZeN' and its planners from *rauminraum*.

USE	- catering
LOCATION	- »Wache 6« in the Forum am Wall in Bremen
HEIGHT	- 4.80 m
USABLE AREA	- approx. 20 sqm
CONSTRUCTION	- steel structure powder-coated, glass façade made of VSG of 2 x ESG, floor coverings: solid oak wood

LUIS AND JORIN'S HIDEAWAY

BREMEN, GERMANY
-

2016

More than ten years ago, my wife and I acquired an old commercial building in Bremen's Steintor district. After closer examination we discovered that the mighty century-old brick ensemble which dominated the interior of the quarter was not worth preserving. We demolished the old building and built a modern new one in its place; now we live and work in it with our two boys. In the space left after demolishing the old building and erecting the new one we created a garden area on the south side with trees and a garden house. The original property was surrounded by a twenty by three metre brick wall. We covered this leftover remnant with a large number of logs. Today, this firewood-covered wall is an an extremely ornamental design element and also functions as an insect hotel as well as comfortable quarters for a few mice. Remarkably, it was only a few years later that we had the idea of building a small house on stilts for our boys Luis and Jorin above the old garden wall. Barely visible, the small house with

its reflecting stainless steel façade now hovers above our garden. A steep staircase leads up to the simple oak clad interior. Here the boys and their friends have their retreat where many a pillow fight has been fought and much hide-and-seek played.

But we adults also enjoy this small space between the leaves of the birch trees very much, for sleeping, reading or simply to cuddle with our children.

TREES - between birches and fan maples

HEIGHT - 3.50 m

STATICS - four supports and frame made of stainless steel

INTERIOR SURFACE - 6 sqm

FAÇADE STRUCTURE - from inside to outside: framework and cladding solid oiled oak, separating foil; RIMEX SuperMirror material: 1.4301 (V2A 0.8 mm)

OVAL
OFFICE

FREUDENSTADT, GERMANY
-
2020

INTERIOR DESIGN: CLIENT

Waldfabrik, a company based in the Black Forest in southwest Germany, develops and produces timeless, handcrafted decoration and gift ideas made of wood. For several years the innovative company has been at home in a beautifully designed commercial office building in Freudenstadt, where it designs and sells its products for the German and the international market.

The desire for an external space for meetings and quiet moments led to the idea of a special and exposed extension to the existing main building. The client's basic idea of connecting a rounded room on columns to the main building via a bridge was the basis on which our planning was to be built. The most important material of the forest factory, wood, led us to the idea of using a twisted (spiral) wood shaving as inspiration for the shape of the room body. After several variants and preliminary studies, the final shape finally developed.

The exact location of the stilt house, taking into account the desired connection to the façade of the existing building, was only one of several challenges encountered during the execution planning as well as during the assembly on the slightly sloping construction site. The partially twisted side terminations of the oval and the transitions of the upper roof surface into the curved underside of the structure were additional details that were not be underestimated and had to be defined.

OVAL
OFFICE

🐦 The bridge, the railings and the supporting horizontal structural plane were created with powder-coated steel profiles. Wood was chosen as the main material for the rounded structure, the cladding of the underside, as well as the inclined supports. The surfaces of the larch supports and the chestnut slats used for the subfloor were treated using a controlled burning technique. This process, known in Japan as 'Yakisugi' and 'Shou Sugi Ban', gives the wood a charming black-ish-silvery surface as well as great durability.

The inside of the oval was covered with a leached and soaped silver fir in contrast to the outer shell. This traditional finish prevents yellowing of the softwood and gives it a light and natural coloration. The builder designed the interior as well as the custom-made furniture and fixtures.

The exterior was also landscaped with new plantings of stately pines, smaller shrubs and a rock garden under the stilt house.

Freudenstadt is almost 800 metres above sea level and snow is not uncommon here in winter. Sitting in the 'Oval Office', the wood-burning stove radiates a pleasant warmth as one looks out through the large glass façades at the snowy landscape of the Black Forest... It could get worse.

FLOOR HEIGHT	7.20 m; roof height 9.80 m
STATICS	bridge and supporting structure steel hollow sections; 9 inclined conical shaped wooden supports made of larch; columns in free arrangement
INTERIOR AREA	lower level 24.0 sqm, upper level 26 sqm
TERRACE AREA	20.4 sqm
TERRACE CONSTRUCTION	steel frame with larch planks
FAÇADE CONSTRUCTION	from inside to outside: 12 mm gypsum board, vapor barrier, 100 mm natural insulation; 100 mm solid wood five-layer boards; underlayment; 20 mm rear ventilation; larch as horizontal formwork
ROOF ROUNDINGS AND EDGES	pre-weathered zinc sheet

GREEN DWELLING

SURROUNDINGS OF HANOVER, GERMANY

–

2019

GARDEN DESIGN: PETRA PELZ AND PETER BERG
INTERIOR DESIGN: GABRIELE EBERT

Our clients, a couple, shared a home with the parents of one of them. The desire of all parties was to create more space and greater design possibilities in their living environment. Through a fortunate circumstance, our clients were able to purchase another piece of land right next to the older home. The approx. 2000 sqm large area with the adjacent forest, the slight slope and a good orientation had promising qualities to realise a new domicile for the younger generation. When first contacting us, our clients were initially interested in building a treehouse on their new property. But soon our task expanded to design not only the treehouse but also the new residence, a very appealing combination of jobs that does not often occur.

The new house should offer as many references to the outside space as possible and at the same time give different retreat possibilities: an oasis in the green with a lot of light, in which the building merges with the garden and becomes one unit, as well as providing a guest room, a sauna area and an enclosed car parking area. A fundamental concern was the ecological quality of the construction and building services. In this regard the desire to use wood as an essential building material was very much to our liking.

A wide variety of designs were presented in the first planning phase including, among other ideas, a floating 'dream room', metallic façades, and both straight and sloping roofs. Ultimately, they were convinced by our proposal to allow the residential building to protrude deep into the site, resulting in a strong fusion of building and outdoor space.

We developed a Z-shaped floor plan, dividing the front part of the building into garage, side rooms and the entrance area. From there one enters the very spacious living room with an open kitchen. In the rear part of the house are the guest rooms, the bathroom, the sauna area and the bedroom. Due to the large glass fronts, each of the rooms have an intense visual relationship and direct access to the garden.

After all the building law hurdles had been cleared and the building permit had been issued, the practical part of the construction could finally begin.

First, large masses of earth had to be moved off the site and load-bearing material had to be moved onto the property. After the foundation work with mainly mineral materials, the construction phase now began with organic building materials.

The entire structure, including exterior and interior walls, as well as the roof and even the floor slab, were built from cross-laminated timber panels. The prefabricated, solid wood components consist mainly of spruce and a layer of larch on the inside. Wood as a natural material was also preferred for the façade. Here, the highly resistant chestnut wood was used in sawn and unedged form.

GREEN DWELLING

SURROUNDINGS OF HANOVER, GERMANY
-
2019

In almost all areas of the interior, the natural, untreated surface of the larch was left visible. In combination with the earthy color of the wood as well as carefully selected furniture, fixed fixtures and textile fabrics, a comfortable but also very modern living atmosphere was created.

The clients had high design requirements not only in the architecture but also in the planning of the garden. After our very rough preliminary planning, the perennial specialist, Petra Pelz, developed a dreamlike garden in cooperation with the outdoor space planner, Peter Berg. Using large natural stone blocks, the garden was terraced and accentuated. A variety of perennials and smaller woody plants were planted in the garden and on the green roof of the building. Already in the first year after creating the outdoor space, the house and garden developed into a harmonious unit and an oasis for the senses. And if you want to have a look at the house and the garden from above, you can go into the treehouse, let your gaze wander and give free rein to your dreams...

LIVING SPACE	-	250 sqm
PROPERTY AREA	-	approx. 2000 sqm
FAÇADE STRUCTURE	-	from the inside to the outside: 100 mm cross laminated timber on the inside larch, 180 mm wood wool insulation, underlay membrane, 40 mm rear ventilation/ battens, floor - cover formwork chestnut rough sawn
ROOF STRUCTURE	-	from the inside to the outside: 240 mm cross laminated timber inside larch, WOLFIN IB roofing and sealing membrane, green roof structure (extensive)
FLOOR	-	oak plank floor, underfloor heating in drywall, insulation, 120 mm cross laminated timber, WOLFIN IB roof and waterproofing membrane on sand bed, STB strip foundations
HEAT GENERATION	-	gas condensing boiler, underfloor heating in dry con struction, controlled living space ventilation The heating requirement is 76.10 kWh / m·a. Standard: EnEV 2016

TREEHOUSE GREEN DWELLING

SURROUNDINGS OF HANOVER, GERMANY
-
2019

The 'Treehouse Green Dwelling' is a treasure which we have integrated into an oak tree on the western boundary of the property. It serves as a family retreat and all-seasonal play space.

The treehouse consists of three flights of stairs, a terrace at a height of four metres and the square treehouse cabin at a height of almost six metres. While the treehouse body rests independently on conically shaped, sloping supports made of glued oak, the terrace is supported by rope suspensions attached to the oak. Highly reflective stainless steel was used as the façade material.

Due to the reflection of the environment on the façade, the 'Treehouse Green Dwelling' appears almost invisible.

The comfortable interior of the treehouse is equipped with upholstered bench and sofa areas, electricity as well as heating. The sofa area can be expanded into a wide king-size bed with mobile elements. Through the very large windows on all façades, the treehouse visitor has an all-round view of the large garden, the residential house with its green roof and into the neighboring forest.

TREES	-	one oak
HEIGHT	-	terrace: 4.0 m; treehouse cabin: 5.5 m
SUPPORTING STRUCTURE	-	7 conically shaped inclined supports made of glued oak wood, supporting frame of the terrace and treehouse as stainless steel, the loads of the terrace structures are transferred to the oak tree without injury by rope structures and belt loops
TERRACE CONSTRUCTION	-	steel frame stainless steel, decking: chestnut
INTERIOR SURFACE	-	8.0 sqm
TERRACE AREA	-	14.4 sqm
FAÇADE CONSTRUCTION	-	from inside to outside: solid oak oiled,18 mm OSB, wooden frame construction with 100 insulation, 18 mm OSB, separating foil; RIMEX SuperMirror material: 1.4301 (V2A 0.8 mm)

DARK ROOM

RUINEN, THE NETHERLANDS
-
2020

☙ The property on the outskirts of the village of Ruinen was used a few years ago completely and exclusively for agricultural purposes. Our client Roel ended his activity as a farmer, renaturalized the land and said goodbye to agriculture.

In the meadows where corn grew and cows grazed, diverse biotopes have evolved over time. Now there are wetlands, flower meadows, hedges and small areas of pristine woods, as well as some ponds where even storks nest in the summer. Within these natural areas, places of art were created, gems full of poetry. It is possible for the residents of the neighbouring community to walk on and enjoy the property. Eventually this place will be frequented by friends and visitors, and offer an open terrain for artistic or other cultural activities. Roel and I approached the treehouse project slowly; after the first contact was made we exchanged information over several phone calls with long intervals in between. Preliminary talks do not necessarily have to last very long for good results, but in this case it was definitely worth it. Our client Roel wanted to dive slowly into the project and accompany every step of the creation of his treehouse with peace and leisure. He needed enough time to define his needs and to find his own approach to the design process.

Thus, more than a year passed before the first meeting and a site visit.

The sheer size and diversity of the property did not make it easy to find the right place for the treehouse. Building code issues, proximity to the home, and subjective impulses had to be weighed against each other.

The shore zone of a large pond seemed to harmonise all wishes and criteria, being still close to the residential house but at the same time not too remote. The stunning view over the meadows and wetlands extended to the adjacent forests on the horizon. Due to the lack of trees in this location, however, it was not possible to create a classic treehouse in the strict sense, but rather a pond house, which didn't matter in the end, given the client's basic requirements. The sensual aspects in the interplay with nature are very similar and very appealing in both cases.

Now began the actual planning: we discussed and evaluated the pros and cons of various designs. When, after a period of collaboration the design was fixed, a feeling of liberation ensued, leaving us with 'only' the technical planning of the object to attend to. Until it came to the assembly of this black room on sloping supports, all components were carefully thought through and prefabricated by our German partner workshops.

The grand finale, the assembly of the house on stilts – or rather the room sculpture – took only three days in midsummer temperatures and went extremely smoothly. During breaks in the assembly we refreshed ourselves in the neighboring natural pond and were well taken care of by Roel and his friends. Thus, the assembly was a great pleasure for all involved and the conclusion of a long and beautiful planning period; a time in which not only an unusual black house was built on sloping supports, but also a time with extremely beautiful encounters and many inspiring moments. Thank you Roel for your trust and our friendship!

The interior, which is tapered on both sides, features a large bed area, angled built-in furniture, a hand basin and a sofa area. All the interior surfaces and built-in furniture were made of oiled oak.

HEIGHT	- lower terrace: 2.8 m; cabin: 4.2 m
SUPPORTING STRUCTURE	- steel supporting structure galvanized and powder coated; seven inclined steel supports under treehouse cabin; four inclined steel supports under terrace.
TERRACE STRUCTURE	- steel structure galvanized and powder coated; decking: sapele wood (FSC certified)
INTERIOR SURFACE	- 10.0 sqm
TERRACE AREA	- 5.4 sqm
FAÇADE CONSTRUCTION	- from inside to outside: solid oak oiled, 18 mm OSB, wood frame construction with 100 insulation, 30 mm rear ventilation, 18 mm OSB, separating foil; RIMEX SuperMirror Black (V2A 0,6 mm),

BLACK CRYSTAL

CATSKILL MOUNTAINS, NEW YORK STATE, USA

-

2020

The Catskill Mountains are characterized by a hilly, partly mountainous topography, large forest areas and agriculture. Smaller cities and towns are connected by small, winding country roads. The world-famous town of Woodstock is also located in this region, which for decades has attracted people who want to rekindle the spirit of the legendary festival.

The Catskill Mountains region is also an attractive recreational area for people from the mega-metropolis of New York City. In little more than two hours by car, the distance is still manageable even for day-trippers. Some of the New Yorkers have built their weekend homes here, an attractive way to escape the intensity of the big city, enjoy nature, clean air and peace, on weekends and vacations.

Kasia and Adam were lucky enough to be able to purchase a beautiful building plot in this now sought-after area. On a large clearing in a wooded area, the family had a modern wooden house planned and built. For a long time, the family members had been big fans of treehouses. At their main residence in New Jersey, building a treehouse is hardly an option. But here on their property in the Catskill Mountains, there's room and lots of trees, too!

Kasia and Adam, both big lovers of edgy and modern architecture, didn't want a traditional treehouse structure built on their property. They wanted a contemporary statement among their trees.

The family discovered our 'Cliff Treehouse' in the media. It was a project we had done a few years earlier, very close by. So Adam contacted us and soon we all enthusiastically began the initial planning steps on both sides of the Atlantic. A few weeks later, I traveled to New York with my colleague Jan Fuchs to inspect the property. We met up personally with Kasia, Adam, their daughter Laika and the family dog Moosky and got an impression of the property. In addition to selecting the building site, we also met Brandon, who would later have a central role in the construction of the treehouse. Not only did our hearts beat to the same drummer in terms of design, we quickly found a shared spark with the entire group. After two intensive days on the property, followed by a short trip to Manhattan where we had a delightful coffee together in autumnal Central Park, Kasia and Adam parted company with us for a few months.

Back in Germany, we quickly set to work. After finalising the design and planning the construction, we decided to produce some of the components in Germany. Brandon and John's team was chosen to manufacture the wooden components and also to assemble the treehouse. We had already had good experiences with these experienced carpenters during the construction of the residential house and had made friends with them.

After about three months of prefabrication, a container carrying the steel components, the windows and the sheet metal for the façade was shipped from Germany to New York. Meanwhile, the regional timber construction company built the foundations, assembled the steel structure and began preparing the timber elements. In October 2019, my colleagues Jan, the accomplished tinsmith Andreas and I, traveled back to NY to the construction site to oversee the rest of the assembly work and finalise the remaining details. Together with the team of John Reidy, Brandon Walsh and John Mocioi, we were able to make great construction progress in an intense week of work. The wonderful team, accompanied by music by Johnny Cash on the construction site, as well as nice and social evenings with Kasia and Adam and their friends made this week an incomparably beautiful experience for all of us.

In the weeks that followed, the façade got finished and the interior was completed by carpenter Catskill Bill. Kasia and Adam refined the black treehouse bit by bit with lovingly selected accessories in the interior and continued with the design of the exterior.

At this point, one must give Kasia and Adam, as well as the local craftsmen, high praise for their work and dedication. For a treehouse of this design results in a multitude of details and great demands on the skills of the craftsmen. Despite never having had to execute them before, the Catskill Mountain team mastered the routines we'd developed working with our German partner companies on many previous projects.

The 'Black Crystal' is finished. Mystical and beautiful.

Kasia, Adam and Laika: enjoy the treehouse! And thanks a lot for the awesome support and your friendship.

BLACK
CRYSTAL

CATSKILL MOUNTAINS, NEW YORK STATE, USA
-
2020

The warm tone of the oak wood in the interior contrasts with the almost aloof black exterior of the treehouse. The walls and roof were clad in a geometric pattern of oak profiles, and the angled lines emphasize the crystal-like character of the project. The fixed sofa can be extended by means of inserts to a large bed area on which the family can sleep comfortably. The gallery can also be used for sleeping, playing and dreaming.

SUPPORTING TREE	- an oak
HEIGHT	- height of terrace: 4.2 m; total height: 8.5 m
SUPPORTING STRUCTURE	- steel structure galvanized and powder-coated; four inclined steel supports under treehouse cabin; the loads of the terrace are supported by steel cables and textile belts from an oak tree.
TERRACE CONSTRUCTION	- steel structure galvanized and powder coated; decking: ipé wood (FSC certified)
INTERIOR SURFACE	- 9 sqm
TERRACE AREA	- 3 sqm
FAÇADE CONSTRUCTION	- from inside to outside: 20 mm solid oiled oak, 21 mm plywood, wood frame construction with 100 insulation, 30 mm rear ventilation, 18 mm OSB, RIMEX SuperMirror Black (V2A 0.6 mm),

TREEHOUSE HOTELS
-
2011–2021

HOTEL EXTENSION
IN MENDOZA

MENDOZA, ARGENTINA
-
2011

A Swiss developer is creating a large spa hotel near the Argentinian city of Mendoza. The hotel aims to offers high standards and will comprise not only the main building but also external accommodation on the property. The idea of building treehouses on this site was impossible owing to the absence of suitable trees. We were asked to design luxury guest accommodation that offers maximum comfort within a small space. The region's intense sunlight and heat during the summer and low temperatures in the winter meant that the buildings would have to feature good shading and good thermal insulation. We designed units consisting of an elliptical cabin with an external terrace situated on several irregularly placed steel columns. A two-flight stairway provides access to the entrance at a height of approximately five metres above ground.

HOTEL
EXTENSION
IN MENDOZA

MENDOZA, ARGENTINA
-
2011

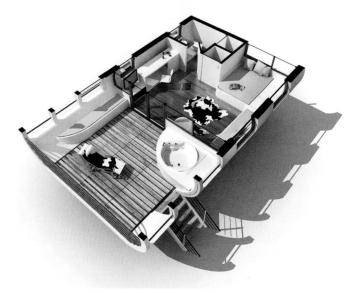

The cabin contains a bathroom, curved couch beds, a desk and minibar. The terrace features a whirlpool where guests can cool off and relax on hot summer days. On a clear day, there is a breathtaking view over the adjacent vineyards of the snow-capped peaks of the Andes.

More information: www.entrecielos.com

'BAUMGEFLÜSTER' TREEHOUSE HOTEL

BAD ZWISCHENAHN, GERMANY

-

2011

Stately trees, a beautiful landscape, a vast selection of leisure activities, and, if possible, a pre-existing infrastructure – a site that provides all of this is a good candidate for hosting a treehouse hotel. When there is a realistic chance of obtaining a building permit, the auspices for success are very favourable indeed. A family from Bad Zwischenahn is the owner of a property that offers all these advantages. In the past, the property was a working farm, but after the end of the farming activities, the family started considering new options for utilising the adjacent forests and the unused parts of the agricultural buildings. The client's ideas initially centred around a complex of four treehouses. In a subsequent development phase, the old farm buildings are to be restored and converted into activity areas. The third phase is to involve the construction of additional treehouses to accommodate extra guests. *Baumraum* developed a design that represented an unusual contrast to the architecture common in this region. The treehouse cabins, each of which is almost 13 metres long, were offset against one another and placed in the forest. While the weight of the cabins rests on 14 irregularly arranged steel columns, each of the treehouse terraces is suspended from a tree. A straight steel stairway provides access to the treehouses, which stand at a height of 3.5 metres above the ground.

'BAUM GEFLÜSTER' TREEHOUSE HOTEL

BAD ZWISCHENAHN, GERMANY
-
2011

❦ The predominant material used for the façades and the interiors is untreated larch wood.
Each treehouse cabin offers a bedroom for two
people, a fully appointed bathroom, and a residential area with a kitchen unit and two additional beds. The white surfaces of the built-in
furniture contrast with the warm tones of the
oiled wood in the interior of the treehouse cabin.

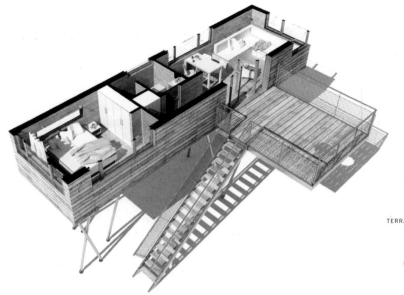

TREES - an oak

HEIGHT - 3.6 m

STATICS - the cabins rest on 14 slanting steel supports in free arrangement; the terrace is suspended from an oak by means of steel cables and stainless steel bolts

TERRACE CONSTRUCTION - untreated larch

TERRACE - 16.4 sqm

INTERIOR AREA - 36 sqm

FAÇADE STRUCTURE - from inside to outside: 20 mm oiled larch boarding; 100 mm five-layer spruce panels; 100 mm DWD–insulation; 20 mm air space; horizontal larch boarding

THE KITCHEN

TULUM, MEXIKO

-

DESIGN 2013

🐾 Christian and his family were on a journey around the world. An extended time out from professional life and our accustomed central European meritocracy often inspires and opens new horizons in their lives. After a few months in North America, the family were bound for the Yucatán Peninsula in Mexico. The small, extremely charming city of Tulum lured them to stay. Acquaintances were made and the idea arose to design and run a restaurant in this heavenly place. 'The Kitchen' was to be the name and slogan of the new location for culinary delights – a restaurant where cooking becomes a spectacle and the preparation of dishes can be experienced first hand. A suitable site between the beach and neighbouring mangrove belt was quickly found. Furthermore, Christian and his partner wanted to build guest accommodation in the form of treehouses on the same site. And so it happened that we received the request to design a restaurant with treehouses in far-away Mexico.

After considering the request for a short time, followed by a few emails and phone calls, I travelled with my team, Cristina Caldieri and Andrea Cigolini, to Tulum. The idea was not only to visit the area, but to prepare the design of the project on-site.

During the ten days of my visit, we lived by the sea and worked on the design in a beach lounge. Our working environment consisted of the surf of the sea, coconut palms and pelicans flying over the water. We might have fared worse! Following discussions with the development team and potentially responsible tradesmen, the design was substantially completed during our stay in Tulum. Only the final artist's impression had to still be created after our visit.

Our concept was divided into a restaurant building that is lined with wood slats, houses built on stilts at the back of the site that overlooks the mangroves and a few smaller adjacent buildings. Seating areas were to be situated outdoors where guests could either enjoy freshly prepared delicacies or a cocktail.

However, after some time the developer notified us that the family's homesickness for good old Germany was greater than anticipated. Thus, for the time being 'The Kitchen' project remains only an artist's impression of a dream representing an escape from reality in Tulum, on the Yucatán Peninsula in Mexico.

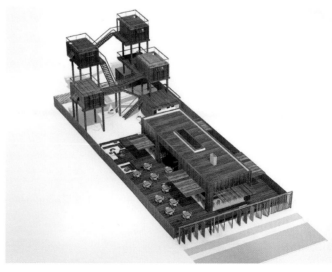

TREEHOUSE LODGE SCHREMS

SCHREMS, AUSTRIA
-
2014

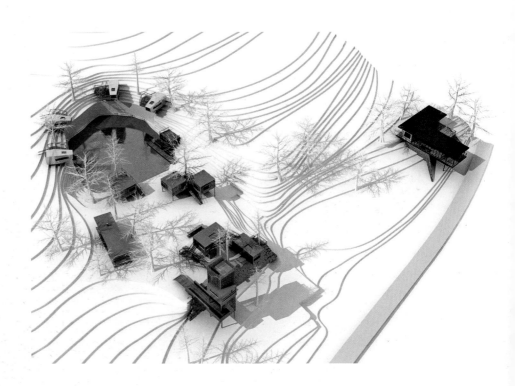

The site for this special construction project is a small wooded property beside an old quarry, right at the eastern fringe of the town of Schrems in Lower Austria. A combination of several happy coincidences makes this site the ideal location for a very special tourism project. The property is surrounded by extensive natural landscapes, but also has the advantage of being located near the town and having tourist attractions in very close proximity. One of these attractions is a lake and the modern underwater theme park *UnterWasserReich* in the *Naturpark Schrems Nature Reserve*.

The property, with its varied character and unique features, is a gem in its own right. At the heart of the site, which covers approximately two hectares, there is an old and long-disused granite quarry. The exposed rock faces rise between two and seven metres above the surface of the little lake that formed after the quarry was abandoned. The vegetation on the property includes several beech and oak trees as well as a few pines and younger spruces. A gully, small hollows and a long natural stone wall lend added interest and variety to the site. An old concrete crane pedestal still stands at its original location. Now overgrown with shrubs, it resembles a monument to the property's history. At the southern boundary, the property gives way to cultivated fields and a grove of birch trees and gives access to a large network of hiking trails. In creating our design, we wanted to respond to the special features of the place and transform its unique spirit into architectural structures. Our strongest impressions of this site were related to the elements of earth, water, and air, which became our guiding principles when developing the design. We divided the property into several different zones:
- the quarry
- the natural stone wall with the crane foundation
- the north boundary with a view of the *UnterWasserReich* theme park
- the gully
- the birch grove on the south side.

TREEHOUSE LODGE SCHREMS

SCHREMS, AUSTRIA
-
2014

❧ Our design calls for a total of four cliff houses at the edge of the quarry. Their angular shape echoes the structure of the rocks. A sauna with a jetty at the level edge of the lake will offer spa facilities for all the guests of the resort. Two treehouses in a large oak tree and a pine tree on the northern side of the lake provide exotic accommodation for additional guests.

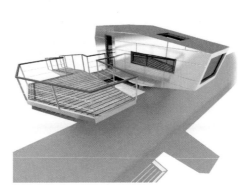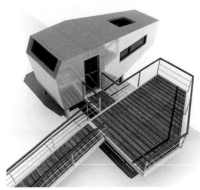

TREEHOUSE LODGE SCHREMS

SCHREMS, AUSTRIA
-
2014

🐾 The reception building, which also contains restaurant facilities, is located at the north-west edge of the property. From this vantage point among birch and pine trees, visitors can enjoy the evening sun, the view of the lake and *Unter-WasserReich* park.

TREEHOUSE LODGE SCHREMS

SCHREMS, AUSTRIA

2014

The residential units above the natural stone wall and old crane foundation, as well as the tower with three accessible floors, were implemented in the first phase of construction. The three buildings were all built with the same materials. The load-bearing structure of the 16-metre high tower was made of galvanised steel sections. The brick house above the wall also rests on low supports and a cantilevered steel frame structure.

One exception is the 'foundation building': On the property there was an old concrete rectangular block. This imposing relict of the recent past probably served as a crane foundation during previous work on a quarry. The charm and tremendous stability of the property led to the idea of using it as a supporting column for a spatial unit. The buildings above the wall and on the base each accommodate a living room, bedroom, bathroom and covered terrace. By contrast, the tower building includes two enclosed living rooms at different levels and an open terrace on the upper platform. From here, guests have a spectacular view of the site, forest and nearby *UnterWasserReich*. Ceilings, walls and floors of all three structures are made of solid prefabricated five-layer spruce panels and have been built with additional insulation. The façade consists of brushed aluminium composite panels which were installed vertically and horizontally. The vertical cladding of the tower staircase is a transparent building envelope made of freshly sawn larch timber beams.

The interiors of all three units provide excellent comfort: a well-appointed bathroom and tastefully decorated living room and bedroom with solid wood furniture. The spruce surfaces of the walls and ceilings have been left visibly in their natural state. Pellet stoves ensure a pleasant climate on cold days.

At the request of Franz Steiner, the developer, the first construction phase of the planning was completed with regional firms under his construction management. Anyone who has ever built a house knows how demanding and gruelling the management of a construction site can be. Franz Steiner himself selected the appropriate construction firms, such as for the complicated steel construction and timberwork. After several months, the first construction phase was completed and the first guests could be received. High praise is due to the developer for his achievement. He has implemented our plans perfectly. We wish him much success with the management of these buildings and already look forward to the subsequent construction phases of this extraordinary project being implemented.

Visit www.baumhaus-lodge.at
for further information

URBAN TREEHOUSE

BERLIN-ZEHLENDORF, GERMANY
-
2014

Experimental construction has long been a tradition at this project location. More than fifty years ago, three acquainted families allowed their homes at this spot to be designed by Heinz Schudnagies, a renowned Berlin architect of organic construction. The grandfather of the developer, Hans-Joachim Stegemann, calculated the statics for this building ensemble, but never built his own home.

The 'Urban Treehouse' is a family project and is based on the initiative of the grandfather Hans-Joachim and his grandson Kolja, who ultimately implemented the project. Once more, it is conceived as an experiment and a research project for new construction and housing in tune with nature. It is intended to serve as an oasis and inspire friends and guests of the family, as well as students and those interested in architecture. We were very enthusiastic when the developer, Kolja Stegemann, approached us with the idea of implementing treehouses in the urban environment of Berlin. Treehouses are normally associated with a rural environment or natural surroundings. Thus, such an undertaking is somewhat rare and very appealing for a planner. In Berlin, one is in good company with regard to small, extraordinary buildings. Here, there are many alternative projects, which often with small budgets occupy niches in the city. As planners, we looked forward to contributing to the tradition of architectural culture in Berlin through this task.

The district of Zehlendorf is characterised by somewhat bourgeois residential buildings with larger properties and gardens. There are not many multi-storey residential buildings here, unlike many other parts of Berlin. The special feature of the site lies in its outstanding location. Bordering the forest, it is located in the immediate vicinity of the beautiful lakes of Krumme Lanke and Schlachtensee. The fact that this land was not built on earlier is surely a stroke of luck and is certainly due to the specific demands of the family.

The treehouses were to cover a relatively small proportion of land. Thus, the usual requirement of using the last available square metre profitably does not apply here. Of course, the preservation of the tree population on the 650 square metre garden property was one of the essential concerns of the developer.

After studying various designs, two cubic units were created – each with 21 square metres of living space. Both buildings hover on a four-metre high base and are equipped with a covered exterior surface at the same height, as well as a lower terrace at a height of 2.60 metres. For one of the treehouses, the intermediate level and both flights of stairs are supported by flexible suspensions from the oak. The building's utilities, supply circuit and storage space for garden tools and waste are located in the base that is lined with larch slats.

The load-bearing design, supports and frame above it consist of galvanised steel sections. Solid prefabricated five-layer spruce panels are used in the walls, ceiling and floor. The advantage of this construction lies in its structural and ecological qualities. These solid wooden parts have a high insulating quality, are breathable, have a high heat storage capacity and can be installed quickly and easily. The rear-ventilated façade consists of aluminium composite panels. Depending on the angle of the light, this can result in a vivid interplay of colour on the outer envelope of the buildings.

The interior provides everything one could possibly need: a bathroom with a shower, a light-flooded interior featuring a kitchenette and comfortable bed, as well as some beautiful home accessories. When it comes to the wall and ceiling panels, the solid wood spruce panels have been left visibly in their natural state.

These treehouses are places that enrapture, inviting one to play and reflect and what is more, to look at things objectively and change perspectives – in other words, these are inspirational places to gather strength. The two treehouses are situated precisely at the transition from city to countryside and thus connect both worlds – vibrant Berlin with restorative scenery.

Shortly before the start of construction, Hans-Joachim Stegemann died in old age. Unfortunately, he was not able to witness the completion of the treehouses and the development of his idea to build something unusual on his land. The treehouses are dedicated to him and his wife. We would like to thank Hans-Joachim Stegemann and his grandson Kolja for this beautiful project.

TREE	- an oak (load-bearing)
HEIGHT	- first level: 2.6 m; second level: 4.2 m
STATICS	- the treehouse cabin is supported by four galvanised steel supports and frames, one of the two lower terrace constructions is suspended from the oak by a system of ropes and webbing loops
TERRACE CONSTRUCTION	- untreated larch
INTERIOR AREA	- 21.0 sqm
TERRACE AREA	- 14.4 sqm
FAÇADE CONSTRUCTION	- from inside to outside: 5 mm aluminium composite panel; 25 mm substructure/air space; 200 mm five-layer spruce panels

TREEHOUSE HOTEL ELBINSELHOF KRAUTSAND

DROCHTERSEN-KRAUTSAND, GERMANY

–

2016

Big ships pass behind the dike and greet you from the Elbe River 500 metres away. In autumn and spring you can listen to the thousands of birds that populate the Elbe island, some year round, some merely stopping here on their way through. At this wonderful place treehouse hotel Elbinselhof Krautsand was realised.

The genesis of this project goes far back into the past. Several years ago our client, Klaus Mayer, had the dream of creating a peaceful spot on a remote pasture at the edge of a forest. In this place, where otherwise horses spent the summer, he wanted to effortlessly retreat – in short, into a treehouse. But then this realisation of his dream fell into oblivion.

Some time later however, in a small bookstore at a gate in Munich Airport, the dream suddenly reappeared in the form of a book entitled *Treehouses* by Andreas Wenning. He bought it, inspired, thus taking the first small step toward the fulfilment of his vision. A little less than a year later, the first project meetings took place and the planning of the treehouses began!

After the completion of the designs for the treehouse facility, a number of discussions with the relevant authorities followed in order to establish a development plan and to submit a building application. After we received the planning permission we built the project with a combination of regional craftsmen and our partners.

The treehouse hotel consists of three large treehouses staggered between a number of old willow trees in front of the earth house. From the treehouse JOJO you have the most beautiful view of the paddocks and the resting places of the wild geese. In the 'first' row are LOTTI and ANNI. Only a horse pasture and the dike separate them from the Elbe.

The treehouses, with timber frameworks, are each supported by 12 sloping steel columns. As a contrast to the rather rectilinear design of the houses, untreated chestnut was used as the façade material. Each of the treehouses has an open terrace on a lower level and a covered outdoor seating area in front of the large glass façade.

TREEHOUSE-HOTEL KRAUTSAND

DROCHTERSEN-KRAUTSAND, GERMANY
-
2016

The interiors equipped with high-quality amenities are made distinctive by the cozy living and sleeping area. In all treehouses there is a pantry, a table group, a sofa corner and a comfortable bathroom. A special element is the inclusion of cozy alcoves, which are integrated into the façades of the houses like bay windows. Oiled oak was used to cover the walls, ceiling, floor and built-in furniture. In the cold season a small wood stove provides the coziness.

TREES	- next to willows
HEIGHT	- two houses: 4.5 m and one house 5.5 m
STATICS	- 12 steel columns support the treehouse cabin, the terrace construction is supported by 4 steel columns.
TERRACE WOOD	- natural chestnut,
INTERIOR SURFACE	- 30.0 sqm
TERRACE AREA	- 18.4 sqm
EQUIPMENT	- bed and bench areas, desk, kitchen, closet, bathroom with toilet and shower
FAÇADE STRUCTURE	- from inside to outside: 20 mm oak boarding oiled; 20 mm OSB; 200 mm insulation; 20 mm OSB, 20 mm rear ventilation/ battening; floor – cover boarding chestnut untrimmed and sawed

THE EARTH
HOUSE

DROCHTERSEN-KRAUTSAND, GERMANY
-
2016

During the planning, the task expanded to include another building; 'Where something so beautiful is built towards the sky, something would also have to be built towards the earth' said the client's partner. This was the beginning of the planning of a complementary earth house.

The earth house was to be built into the side of an existing hill, made long ago of dirt dumped over an old building. During the planning it turned out, however, that it is one of the oldest historical mounds in Krautsand from the 16th century and it is therefore protected as an archaeological monument. Without further ado, we decided to build a new dwelling next to it and to erect the earth house inside it.

The load-bearing construction consists mainly of concrete. Laterally sloping walls hold the earth in the large glass façade facing west and form the frame to the terrace area and the entrance area. This rather cool material was left visible in the surfaces of the interior, ceiling and side walls. Nevertheless, the combination with the oak floor and rear partition creates a minimalist yet warm character. In a central location, the room receives additional daylight from above through a prismatic roof opening. At the back of the ground room is a small kitchen, a toilet and a technical room.

This simple but special room is used as a meditation, yoga or seminar room.

LIZARD

HORSESHOE BAY, DIKWELLA, SOUTHERN PROVINCE, SRI LANKA

-

DESIGN 2017

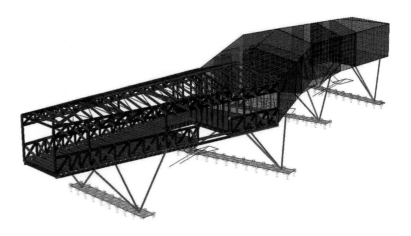

Niall, a young Australian, discovered the south of Sri Lanka with his German girlfriend Maggi during a trip, fell in love with the country and started his own backpacker hostel on the south coast of the tropical island. After only a short time, his hostel Hangtime became a hot spot for the international backpacker scene.

The ambitious Australian had the idea to expand his touristic offer with exquisite accommodation made by creating and building high quality treehouses. The search for a suitable property proved to be not so easy here either. Even in this part of the world, attractive building plots close to the coast are not easy to come by and are usually very expensive. Therefore, the piece of land selected by Niall, an hour's drive east of Hangtime Hostel, was a particular stroke of luck, despite its very narrow layout. With dimensions of approx. 52 x 12 metres, the narrow plot bordered almost directly onto the sea and, with its immediate proximity to dreamlike beaches such as Horseshoe Bay, was the basis for further planning.

Due to Maggi's German origin and passion for modern architecture, Niall contacted us and visited us during a trip to Germany in Bremen. At the first joint meeting, a very friendly atmosphere quickly developed. Also in design questions our

hearts beat equally close to each other. Keeping the underground as light as possible and using energy resources as sparingly as possible in the construction and operation of the building, were to be important parameters in the planning. Commissioned with the design planning, we set to work and then presented various concepts.

Contrary to the first idea to develop smaller units on the property, the client was most convinced by our proposal to realise a coherent building, which should combine the accommodation and the restaurant under one roof. Within this basic idea, there were then various sub-variants that were compared with each other.

The design, nicknamed 'Lizard', had the greatest appeal for Niall and us and was to be developed further in the subsequent planning. The favored concept was characterized by a zigzag-shaped building floating on sloping supports. The lower level houses the bar, kitchen and ancillary rooms, as well as the swimming pool on the side facing the Indian Ocean. The lush tropical greenery of the garden was to be seamlessly routed under the building, enveloping the private rest areas and outdoor showers.

The upper part of the wooden structure houses the four apartments for guests, accommodation

for employees and the covered restaurant area with a sea view. While the narrow load-bearing columns were intended to be made of coated steel, the entire floating part of the building was to be realised in timber construction. For the entire façade of the upper part of the house, the branches of the regionally grown cinnamon plant were intended. Our concept was then screened from a structural point of view by our structural engineers FS1 from Innsbruck and the main components were dimensioned.

Our planning and the preliminary considerations for the execution of this plan were then to be implemented by a regional architect and local craftsmen. Niall invited me to visit Sri Lanka to inspect the building site and to better understand the regional possibilities.

A charming offer which I of course gladly accepted. However, I did not want to undertake this trip to this exotic and dreamlike destination without my wife and our two boys. For our two boys such a long journey almost to the equator was a great adventure.

Niall helped us choose accommodations and put together a selection of excellent destinations on the south coast of Sri Lanka. So the whole family flew to South East Asia for the Easter vacations.

During the two weeks of our stay we met possible partners for the realisation of the 'Lizard' and explored regional building techniques and materials. In our free time we enjoyed the beautiful Indian Ocean, the food and the very friendly inhabitants of the island. We toured gorgeous landscapes and saw exotic animals such as wild elephants. We had an impressive and beautiful trip. A trip with many experiences that our children still like to talk about today.

In this part of the world, too, the destruction of natural areas and extreme environmental pollution is conspicuous and very worrying. This sad realisation was confirmed to us at first hand on this trip. Tourism, with its encroachment on ever more natural areas, is making a significant contribution to this development. Against this background, the involvement of an architect in the development of such projects is not unproblematic and can only be justified if natural resources are handled

sensitively and responsibly. I hope that our design has been able to meet these necessary parameters. Unfortunately, the realisation of the very fancy design has not taken place up until today. Questions of building law and economy have delayed or questioned the start of construction so far. We will gladly travel to this beautiful country again and hope to stay overnight in the 'Lizard' and to jump into the wonderful Indian Ocean in the neighboring Horseshoe Bay.

TREEHOUSE HALDEN

HALDEN, SWITZERLAND
-
2017

☙ Realising a dream sometimes entails a lot of endurance and willpower.

Longtime friends Helgard and Nina had a vision of their own treehouse several years before the project was tackled and the first plans were on the table. They wanted to create a special hideaway for themselves and for their guests. Helgard also wanted to use the space occasionally for her psychotherapeutic practice, so the basis of this project was the synergy of private passions and professional practicality.

The family property in the Swiss village of Halden near Lake Constance (situated where Germany, Switzerland, and Austria meet), dotted with a few beautiful oak trees, was perfect for this unusual building project. The family's timber-framed house, located on the property, effortlessly provided the building's utilities as well as a place for entertaining guests.

During the planning process, several studies suggesting roof shapes, façade materials and floor plan variants were developed and evaluated. After careful consideration, they settled on an almost black building whose design (despite the inclusion of a gabled roof) was both clear and modern, including large glass surfaces and linear details in the outer shell as well as in the interior fittings. After a period of building code formalities, all components were prefabricated in Germany. The on-site assembly was then carried out by a larger team within just a few days.

The assembly was physically demanding on the German team, requiring long working days, but lightened by the intensive and beautiful cooperation within the assembly team and by the great hospitality of the two builders Helgard and Nina, who always knew how to spoil everyone with their excellent cuisine. These assembly days became a particularly happy and eventful experience for the team of craftsmen and the two clients, which will certainly remain in good memory for a long time.

TREEHOUSE HALDEN

HALDEN, SWITZERLAND
-
2017

The small house in the trees is defined by the openness of the living room and bedroom provided by the glass gable on the north side which allows a lot of light into the interior and opens a picturesque view over an orchard of the small valley down to the river Thur.

Oiled oak was used for the cladding of the walls, the ceiling, the floor and the built-in furniture, giving the interior a calm, homogeneous character. Above the integrated pantry and bathroom is a gallery with a cozy sleeping area. From here, through a skylight, you have a view of the treetop of the neighboring oak tree and on a clear night, of the stars. A small wood stove provides warmth and coziness on cold days. Highlights of the tidy, compact bathroom are the concrete-like surface of the shower and sink made of natural stones which were carefully selected from the neighboring river. A stonemason shaped the large pebbles into stone tops for the wood furniture.

TREES	- an oak
HEIGHT	- 4.2 to 5.5 m
STATICTS	- steel frame with four wooden supports under the treehouse cabin; the treehouse terrace is supported by the oak using rope structures and belt loops
TERRACE CONSTRUCTION	- steel structure, terrace boards made of untreated chestnut
FAÇADE STRUCTURE	- from the inside to the outside: 20 mm oak formwork oiled; 20 mm OSB; 100 mm wood wool insulation; 30 mm ventilation/ battens; floor - cover formwork in larch, rough sawn black varnished
INNER SURFACE	- 22 sqm
TERRACE AREA	- 14 sqm

LÜTETSBURG TREEHOUSE LODGES

LÜTETSBURG BEI NORDEN, GERMANY

-

2019

At the beginning of 2013, I met Tido Graf zu Inn- und Knyphausen for the first joint inspection on his estate in Lütetsburg. To begin with, we walked through the beautiful castle park which, with its impressive tree population, seemed to be a very attractive place for treehouses. Mr Graf Knyphausen then showed me the grove at the back of the golf course. The remoteness of the place and the fantastic view over the gently rolling landscape convinced us both immediately, and all other options quickly faded into the background. After comparing different preliminary designs for the treehouse complex, a modern interpretation of the traditional gable roof house with an almost black façade crystallised.

This was followed by a number of discussions with the relevant authorities, which led to the drawing up of a development plan. Since the procedure turned out to be very complicated in parts, the construction of the treehouses could not begin until the summer of 2018 after five years of preparation.

The treehouse complex created there consists of three large stilt houses on the southern edge of a small wood, surrounded by gently rolling meadows, the adjacent golf course, hedges, small groups of trees and the typical East Frisian landscape with great distant views.

The three stilt houses were carefully integrated into the existing tree population with their prominent gable façades facing South. The wooden houses and the terraces rest on a steel structure with partly straight and partly sloping supports.

A dark anthracite was chosen for the outer shell. This colour is found on the larch wood cladding, the windows and the metal roof covering.

The idea of providing the large glass surfaces with a branch graphic was developed together with responsible nature conservationists. In addition to the aesthetic effect, the graphic is primarily intended to allow birds to visually perceive the transparent surfaces and thus prevent the animals from colliding with them.

LÜTETSBURG
TREEHOUSE
LODGES

LÜTETSBURG BEI NORDEN, GERMANY
-
2019

☙ Each of the treehouses has an open terrace on a lower level, as well as a covered balcony on the gable end. From here one can best enjoy the landscape and not infrequently observe a variety of wildlife such as fallow deer, hares and various species of birds.

The interiors of the stilt houses are notable for the untreated larch wood on the wall and roof surfaces, as well as anthracite-coloured fixtures. On the first level there is the spacious living and dining area, a small bedroom with a bunk bed for two people, an exclusively equipped bathroom and a foyer area including a wardrobe.

Amenities include a fully functional kitchenette with dining table, a seating area with sofa and WiFi access. The geothermal-based underfloor heating and the well-insulated exterior shell provide warmth and comfort even on cold days. The open gallery with the sleeping area on the second level provides a special experience for guests. Here they can enjoy spectacular views of the treetops and open countryside through the large expanses of glass.

The patrons of the three houses are the fox, the badger and the deer. They welcome guests right at the entrance door and get visitors in the mood for a special stay with a lot of comfort in the middle of nature.

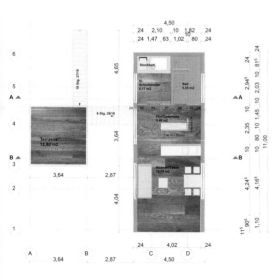

	SURROUNDING TREES	- mixed woody plants (oaks, beeches, alders, birches and conifers)
SUPPORTING STRUCTURE	- steel frame structure with 4 vertically arranged supports in the rear area and 4 obliquely arranged steel supports in the front area; the terrace structure is supported by 4 steel columns
HEIGHTS ABOVE GROUND	- first terrace: 3.0 m, living level: 4.2 m, sleeping level: 6.8 m, ridge: 10.0 m
INTERIOR AREA	- 54 sqm
TERRACE AREA	- 14 sqm
FAÇADE STRUCTURE	- from the inside to the outside: 100 mm cross laminated timber inside larch, 120 mm wood wool insulation, underlay, 40 mm rear ventilation / lathing, floor-ceiling boarding larch sawed with glaze color anthracite
FLOOR CONSTRUCTION	- from the inside to the outside: tiles, 55 mm screed / floor heating, 100 mm insulation, 160 mm cross laminated timber
ROOF STRUCTURE	- from inside to outside: 100 mm cross laminated timber , 120 mm wood wool insulation, underlay, 40 mm air layer, 22 mm OSB, zinc roofing
HEAT GENERATION	- central geothermal heat pump with local heating network, underfloor heating

LUG IN LAND

ILSENBURG (HARZ), GERMANY

-

DESIGN 2019/2020
REALISATION 2021

Not least because of the changed climate situation in the low mountain ranges and in the alpine locations, new concepts in the tourism industry had to be invented. The quality of accommodation and the proximity and integration of nature can be important factors in the development of tourism concepts.

In some areas of the Harz Mountains, a highland area in northern Germany, the offer of attractive accommodation that take into account the changing needs of vacationers is still expanding.Our developers have recognised this development potential and have acquired a natural building plot near Harz National Park in the small town of Ilsenburg in the northern Harz Mountains.

After extensive preliminary research and visits to other treehouse hotels, we were commissioned with the planning of a stilt house facility on the selected property.

The clarification of the building law almost always requires a lot of patience and time for such building projects. In the case of this project, we must pay a special compliment to the client-couple for their commitment and persistence. Together with a regional planning office and us, the clients had to hold extensive discussions with the various authorities and other parties involved, clarify formalities and clear up imponderables until the necessary legal framework was

created in the form of a development plan and the final building permit was on the table. On the east-facing hillside site, the plans envisage six almost identical houses and a utility building. The buildings are to be strongly embedded in the greenery of the existing trees on the edges of the site, as well as in the neighboring forest on the west side and embedded also in further new on-site plantings of native woody plants. Largely constructed of cross-laminated timber, each of the houses rests on a laterally placed base and two slender steel columns. The construction of the houses is based on the use of cross-laminated timber as a structural as well as visible material on the inside. The natural character of the complex is supported by the use of untreated larch wood on the façades of the buildings.

Contemporary energy standard requirements are to be met by strong wood-wool insulation on the outside of the cross-laminated timber components and by the use of a central geothermal heat pump via an underfloor heating system.

All houses have both open and covered terraces, combined living and dining areas and separate bedrooms with space for a whole family. With a small sauna located in the plinths under the houses, guests in 'Treetop – Resort Lug ins Land' will also be able to sweeten their stay in the winter.

TRIFELS

ANNWEILER, GERMANY

-

DESIGN 2021
REALISATION 2022

Trifels, the art nouveau hotel in the middle of the dreamlike nature of the Palatinate Forest, with a view of the castles Trifels, Anebos and Münz, is an ideal starting point for hiking tours.

The historic Kurhaus is a location where weddings and family gatherings are celebrated, seminars and conferences held, and vacations spent. Both the kitchen and the fully renovated, high-quality designer rooms offer guests a setting that leaves nothing to be desired.

Due to the scarce capacity of rooms and the difficulty of extending the listed building, the clients were looking for new concept ideas to expand the hotel business.

In the immediate vicinity of the Kurhaus is a sloping meadow directly on the edge of the forest. Hiking trails and wooded strips bump up against the property on the partial side at the edge of a stream as well as on the sides. As the community had already designated the property as an extension to the hotel, the client decided to create the extension with carefully integrated architecture, making nature available for the enjoyment of his guests. The spacious stilt houses we planned are located directly

at the edge of the forest and have large glass fronts facing the valley. Depending on the topography, the staircases as well as the supporting structure of the three houses vary in orientation and height.

All houses have both open and covered terraces, a combined living and dining area and a separate bedroom at the back. On the second level there is a gallery for sleeping and playing with a view through the large glass gable into the meadow and tree landscape.

High above, just across the street, towers Trifels Castle. Not a bad view!

K1

ODENTHAL, GERMANY

-

DESIGN 2020 / 2021
REALISATION 2021 / 2022

The conditions were optimal for a successful treehouse hotel project: A fantastic plot of land at the gates of Cologne, located in the beautiful nature of the Bergisches Land with a beautiful tree population, a good pre-existing, usable infrastructure of the high ropes course K1, as well as the existence of a legally binding development plan for a treehouse hotel in total provided a very good basis for our work as planners.

In addition, Stefan Vornholt is an ambitious client with a great passion for treehouses who, as the operator of the K1 climbing forest, had already gained a lot of experience with trees and their environmentally friendly use.

For ages, the climbing forest and its entire tree population has been expertly cared for by the tree expert, Martin Zeller. This was a happy coincidence since I had met Martin a few years ago at another treehouse project near Basel and appreciated his expert knowledge greatly. Zeller is a professional specialist in the assessment of trees which are exposed to extraordinary loads, e.g. by technical facilities (treehouses, platforms, treetop paths, climbing elements etc.). Furthermore, he developed special implants for the introduction of artificial loads into living trees. Martin Zeller teaches the course 'Tree Engineering' at the Faculty of Architecture and Civil Engineering at the Technical University in Dortmund.

The Chair of Statics and Dynamics in Dortmund, headed by Prof. Ingo Münch, is scientifically concerned with the static and dynamic modeling of living trees.

The ambitious goal is to incorporate this know-how into the K1 project and to support us in the planning of the storage, as well as in the static calculation of the supporting trees for the treehouses. Based on the experience gained so far by the engineers involved and by us, the trees surveyed are to bear heavy loads without us interfering with the natural habitat. Even after completion of the treehouses, the effects of the bearing and load application on the supporting trees are to be evaluated and scientifically accompanied by the students of the Dortmund University of Applied Sciences and Arts.

The underlying development plan specified the number of 6 treehouses or stilt houses as well as their maximum size and locations on the forest plot. On the first site, a small tree-independent house should be created, while on the other sites, we aim to completely or partially attach the treehouses to the selected supporting trees.

On this basis we have designed six very different treehouses. The designs vary in their basic shape, in the choice of materials, in their height and in the number of usable levels. Some of the treehouses will be connected with bridges and footbridges and thus fit in well with the nearby climbing forest.

We are looking forward to the realisation with a promising team at this very beautiful location, and to test sleeping in each of the treehouses.

BAUMRAUM VISIONS

THE FOLLOWING PAGES CONTAIN VARIOUS FICTIONAL BAUMRAUM VISIONS. THESE TREEHOUSE VISIONS WERE DESIGNED FOR VARIOUS DIFFERENT LOCATIONS AROUND THE WORLD. THE COMBINATION OF UNUSUAL SETTINGS AND CONTEMPORARY DESIGN AIMS TO STIMULATE THE OBSERVER'S IMAGINATION AND HIGHLIGHT A VARIETY OF POSSIBILITIES FOR EMBEDDING THESE STRUCTURES IN NATURAL SETTINGS. EACH DESIGN IS BASED ON A BASIC CONCEPT FROM WHICH FINER DETAILS ALMOST INEVITABLY FOLLOW. WHILE ALL THESE DESIGNS ARE CHALLENG-ING TO PLAN AND EXECUTE, IMPLEMENTING THEM IS NEVERTHE-LESS A REALISTIC POSSIBILITY.

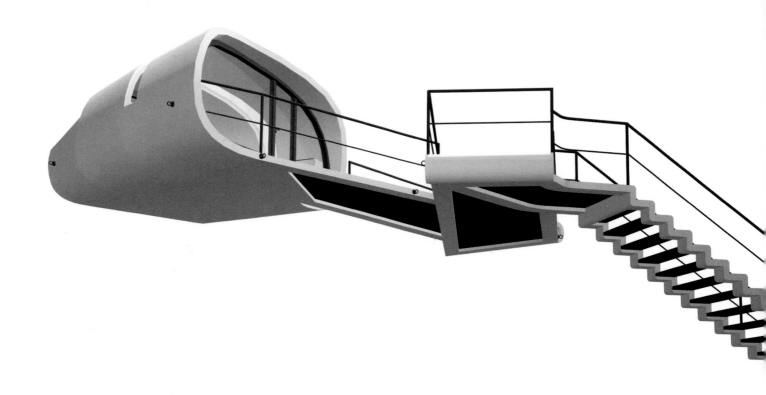

  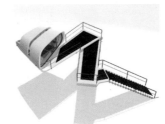 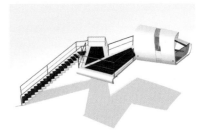

LOOP

-

PLANNING TIME 2008

The point of departure for this concept is 'folding'. Thanks to its three-dimensional development, the staircase turns into a ramp and defines the floor, wall, and ceiling space of the treehouse. Owing to the meandering surfaces, a tension is created in the path between the trees. Furthermore, there is a seamless transition to the interior space. The approach which embodies the design is evident not only in the exterior building elements.

LIGHTNING

—

PLANNING TIME 2008

With its sharp-edged contours, dynamic expression and austere use of shape, this design is not for those who prefer cosier surroundings. This treehouse literally shoots through the woods like a bolt of *lightning*, its corners and edges moving through the trees. A long ramp rises upwards to the treehouse cabins and serves as an adventure trail between the tree trunks. The ramp divides the treehouse into two sculpturally shaped corpuses, becoming a terrace at the end. The two corpuses house the sleeping quarters on the one hand, and an open living space with a small wet area on the other. Separated only by a sheet of glass, the smoothly designed interiors flow into a covered open-air seating area. The crystalline appearance of the design is further evidenced in the structure of the metallic façade elements and the glass areas.

CONE TREEHOUSE

-

PLANNING TIME 2008

A cone provided the formal idea for this design. The concept foresees that the cone-shaped treehouse is penetrated by a large coniferous tree and rests on this without additional supports. Depending on the height and size of the tree, the treehouse may be fitted with a second, mid-level terrace. Access is via a spiral staircase which ends in a floor hatch on the underside of the treehouse. The façade is clad in cedar shingles and fitted with metal-framed windows and doors. Inside, there are two levels with sleeping quarters, a small bathroom and the living room.

WINDING SNAKE

-

PLANNING TIME 2008

The *Sequoia sempervirens*, also known as the coast redwood, is native to the North Californian forests, stretching as far as South Oregon. These giant trees reach heights of over one hundred metres and can live for more than two thousand years. The design of the 'Winding Snake' is situated on this type of tree. The treehouse comprises a staircase which winds like a snake around a mighty sequoia trunk, ending in a twin-storey cabin. At mid-height there is an elliptically-shaped terrace. The weight of the construction is transferred to textile straps via steel cables. The dimensions of these trees allow them to bear considerably greater weights than this.

WINDING SNAKE

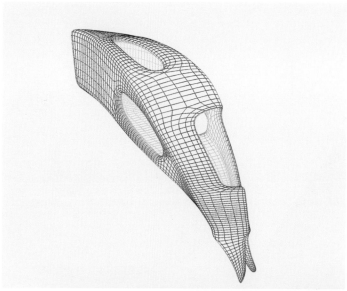

PALM FICTION

-

PLANNING TIME 2008

The South Seas ... golden sandy beaches, warm, clear water, a permanently blue sky, and, naturally, many palm trees. I am enjoying a Martini-on-the-Rocks, or perhaps a White Russian five metres above the ground on my terrace, which sways between the coconut palms. The palm leaves provide pleasant shade. My eyes gaze towards the sea, while my senses luxuriate in the soothing sound of the waves. The sun slowly drops on the horizon and disappears into the sea with a breathtaking display of colours. It grows dark, but it is still very warm. Perhaps another drink or two? Barely definable animal noises from the adjacent forest blend with the endless sound of the sea. Black night falls, and I climb up a few steps higher to my cocoon in the palms. I leave the windows open and a gentle breeze ripples through the curved interior. The glass dome of my little kingdom affords a view of the firmament. Everything sways gently and my body is overtaken by drowsiness.

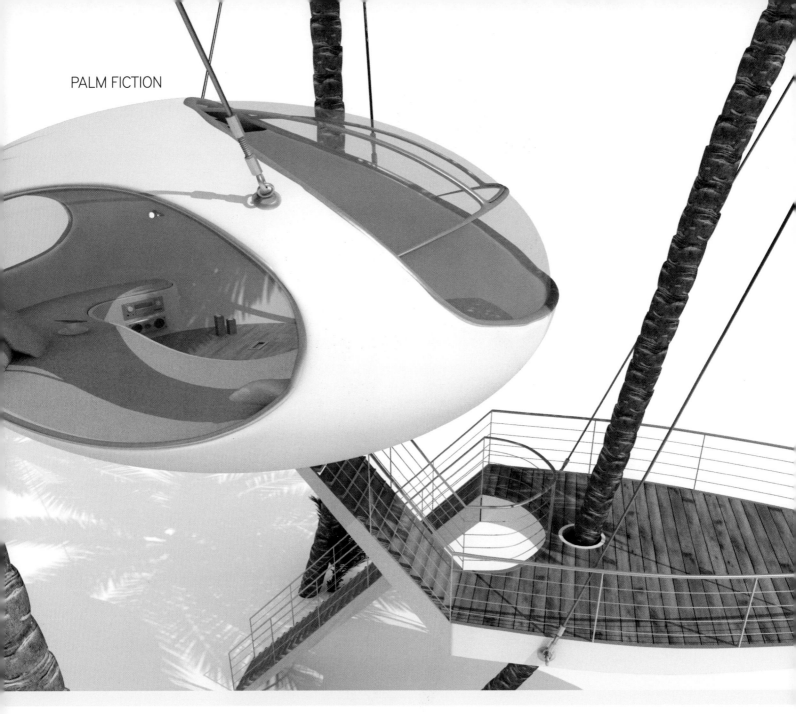

JUNGLE HOUSE

-

PLANNING TIME 2008

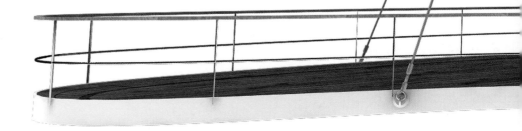

The 'Jungle House' is a luxurious version of a tree-house. It has brilliant white, organically-shaped architecture and an extremely comfortable interior. The space, with its curved walls and ceilings, is oriented to the sea or perhaps to a river on the edge of the tropical rainforest. It could also be on a mountain slope, opening itself up to a valley.

The weight of the treehouse rests on several slender supports. Only the terrace is supported by a tree or palm. The 'Jungle House' is a fully functional living unit, furnished to a high standard. The living area contains a sitting and reclining area, as well as a whirlpool. This central room leads into the outdoor terrace opposite.

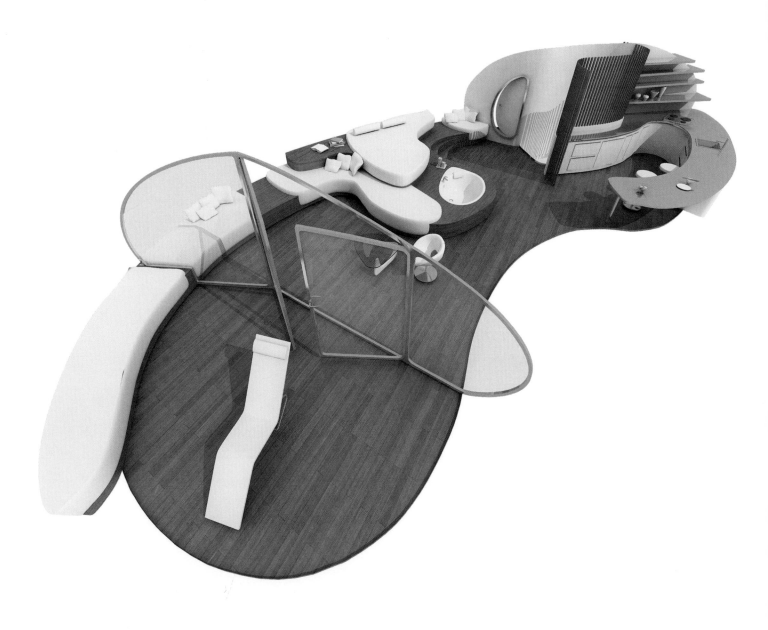

WATER LILY

-

PLANNING TIME 2008

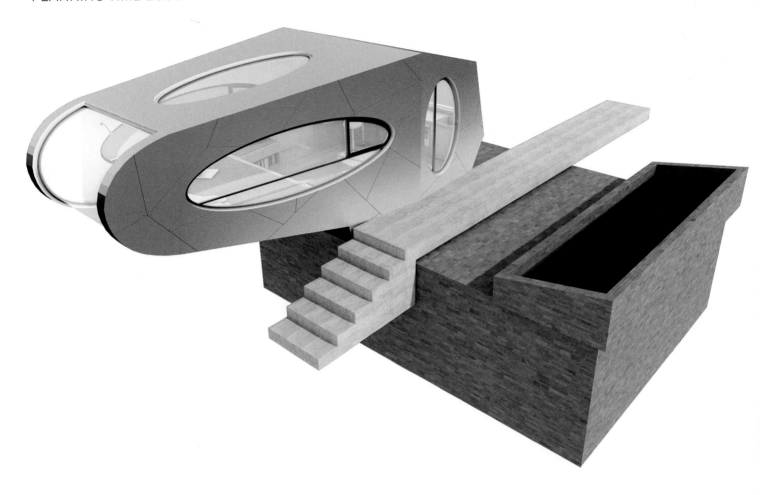

Trees, water, and earth are the determining elements of this design. The location for the 'Water Lily' is a tranquil expanse of water, the shores of which are lined with trees and bushes. This small construction comprises two parts of very different character. The section of the building visible from outside is situated on the shoreline. It literally rises up from the greenery and leans far out over the surface of the lake.

The façade of this dynamically shaped corpus is fitted with metal plates and oval windows. The interior is flooded with light and contains a small kitchen, plenty of storage space and a sleeping area which 'floats' above the water. From here, there is an enchanting view of the lake and tree-tops through the circular window. A narrow stair-case leads to the second area of the building. This is concealed in the earth, barely visible, and is

entirely dedicated to water and tranquillity. It contains a small sauna and relaxation area. A longitudinal ceiling opening provides daylight into this otherwise windowless space. The light falls on the pool and large shower fixtures. The introverted effect of this space is underlined by the use of natural stone throughout. The pool is fed by lake water. Those who want to enjoy the water can do so via an outdoor staircase.

BENEATH THE LEAVES

–

PLANNING TIME 2008

This design is dedicated to the hidden part of trees. Beneath the forest floor there is a sub-structure of organically-shaped spaces which connect to each other in a variety of ways. From outside, this subterranean living world is only visible through the flatly curved dome lights. Access is via various points, which are integrated almost invisibly into the floor of the forest. At first glance, this design has a somewhat mystical aura. The sinister image of a cave is softened by the bright surfaces of the interior spaces and the natural light which enters through the glass domes. A very special living experience has been created which offers unusual perspectives of the tree-tops and sky.

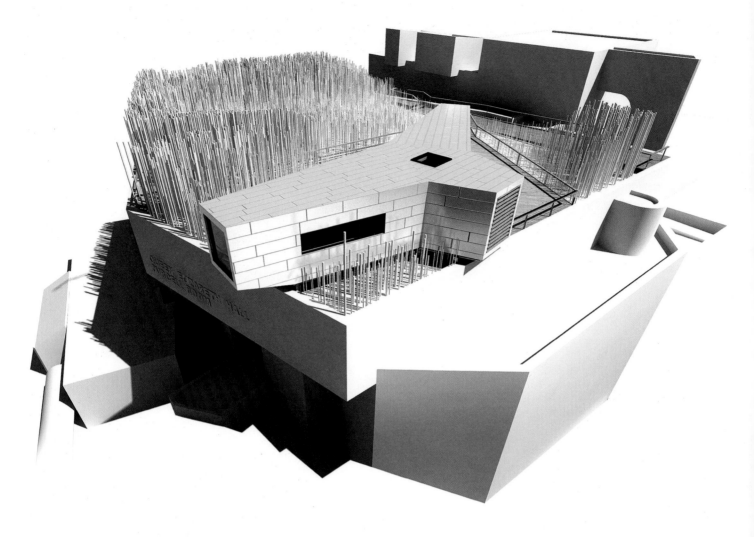

ON THE ROOF

LONDON, UK, ON THE ROOF OF THE QUEEN ELIZABETH HALL

-

PLANNING TIME 2010

'Parasitic architecture' is a technical term that typically denotes small spaces that are added onto – or implanted into – an existing building or structure. This addition benefits from the support structure of the 'host' building and makes use of its existing infrastructure, such as building services, electricity and water. A treehouse is an example of 'parasitic architecture' since without the tree, the treehouse could not exist. A building may host such 'parasitic' spaces on its façade, in its interior, or even on its roof. Organisers from Great Britain chose to single out this intriguing subject and launch an architectural competition. Architects from all over the world were invited to develop suggestions for a hotel suite on the roof of the Queen Elizabeth Hall. The purpose of this exotic location is to offer tourists a very special, high-standard hotel experience for a brief period of time. In addition to submitting an architectural design, competitors were required to present their ideas for the exterior design of the rest of the roof. *Baumraum* rose to the challenge in late 2010 and submitted an entry.

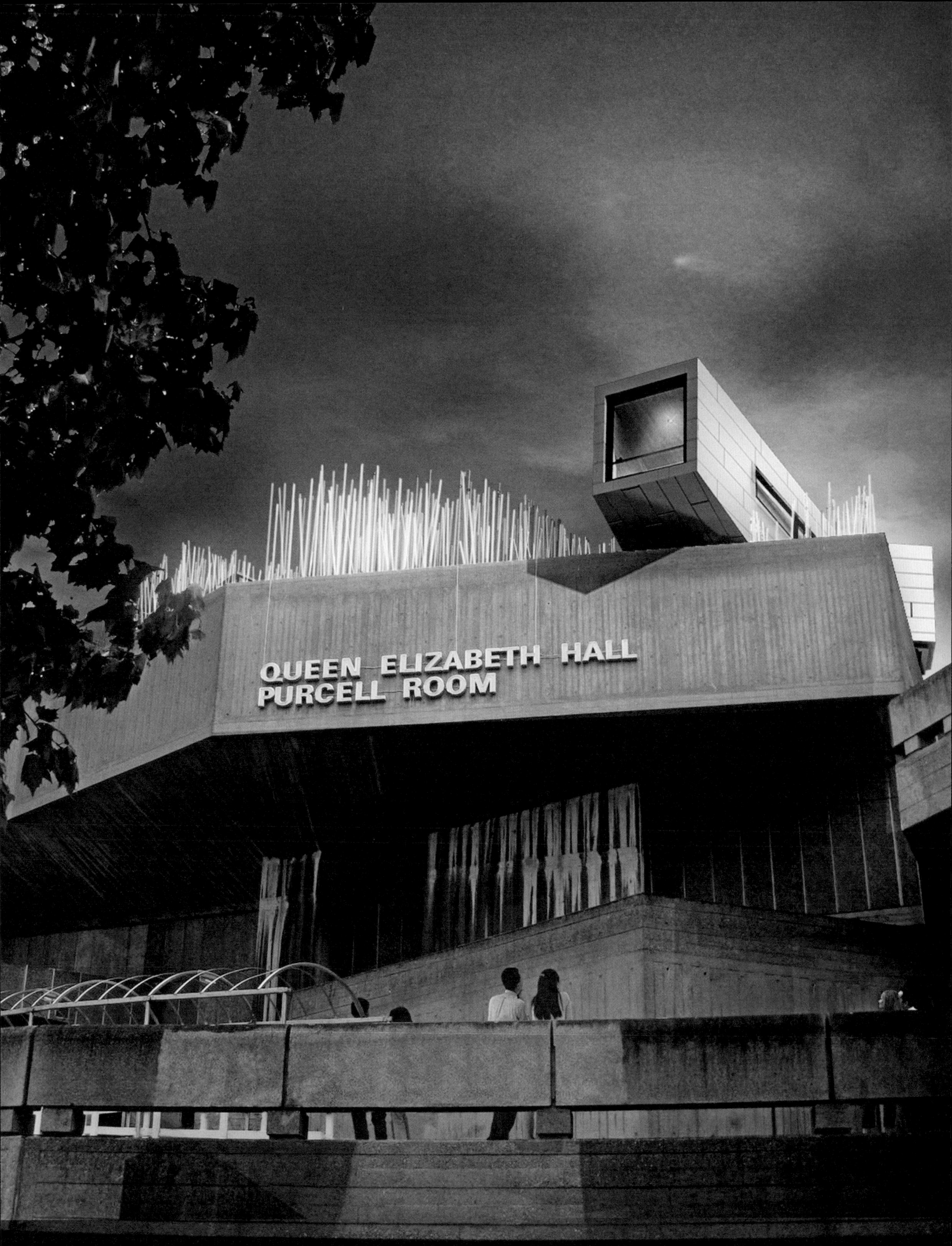
QUEEN ELIZABETH HALL
PURCELL ROOM

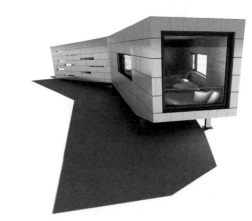

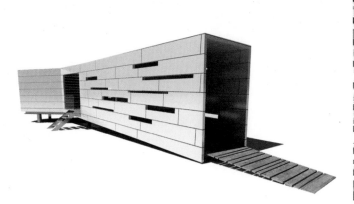

Our suggestion takes the form of an elongated, crystal-shaped structure. A diagonal route from the roof exit of the concert hall brings visitors to a ramp that leads into the tunnel-like entrance-way. The interior of the suite contains a foyer, bathroom and the living and sleeping area. The windows were deliberately placed to provide a view of the city's major landmarks. From here, visitors would have had a breathtaking view across the Thames to the London Eye, Big Ben, and the Houses of Parliament. A sea of plastic fluorescent tubes was to be installed on the exterior. Over 500 architecture firms from various countries submitted designs for this competition. Sadly, *Baumraum* did not have the good fortune to emerge victorious from this large field of competitors. However, creating the design was an intriguing challenge.

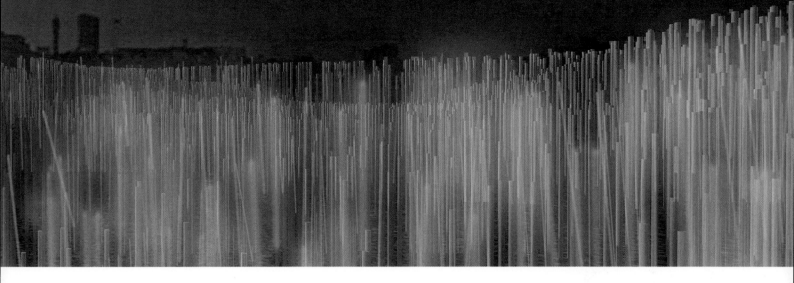

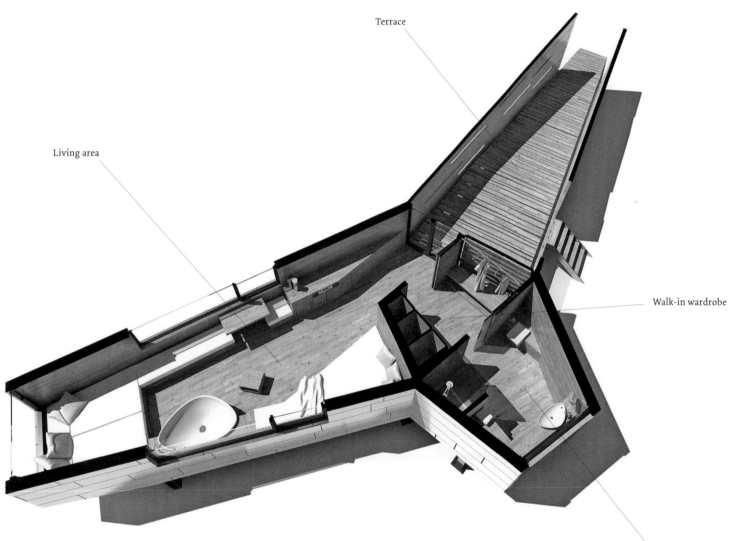

Terrace

Living area

Walk-in wardrobe

Bathroom

PARTNERS

Many thanks to our partners in implementing the projects.

PERMANENT PARTNERS

Tischlerei Heidhoff & Helms GmbH
D-27305 Bruchhausen-Vilsen
www.tischlerei-heidhoff.de

Peter Rundi Elektrotechnik
D-28816 Stuhr

Schorling wood construction
D-27211 Bassum-Dimhausen
www.schorling-holz.de

Carpentry Lars-Tino Bobek
D-27211 Bassum
www.bobek-moebel.de

Metal construction Heinrich Günnemann
D-27211 Bassum
www.guennemann-metallbau.de

Carpentry Rüdiger Abel und Bernd Hoock
D-69469 Weinheim
www.abel-innenausbau.de

Norddeutsches Draht- und
Seil-Kontor A. Cordes e.K.,
D-28199 Bremen
www.drahtseil-cordes.de

JWD roof and façade engineering
D-49406 Eydelstedt
www.jwd-dach.de

Foam center
D-28201 Bremen
www.schaumstoff-center.de

FTF Fensterbau
27211 Bassum
www.ftf-fenster-tueren-fassaden.de

Dipl.- Ing. Matthias Jesske
D-28879 Grasberg

Baumrausch, Alexander Grote
D-37581 Bad Gandersheim
www.baumrausch.de

Baumbüro, Dipl.-Ing. Klaus Schöpe
D-26188 Edewecht-Wittenberge
www.baumbuero.de

Martin Zeller
D-79356 Eichstetten
www.Baumzentrum-Kaiserstuhl.de

Ingenieurbüro Helfried Schmitz
D-28203 Bremen
www.statik-schmitz.de

FS1 Fiedler Stöffler Ziviltechniker GmbH
A-6020 Innsbruck
www.fs1-gmbh.at

Ingenieurbüro Braun GmbH & Co. KG
75179 Pforzheim
www.braun-ing.de

Prof. Dr.-Ing. Ingo Münch
Lehrstuhl Statik und Dynamik, TU Dortmund
www.tu-dortmund.de

Rimex Metals (Deutschland) GmbH
www.rimexmetals.com

PROJECT-RELATED PARTNERS

Hausinholz, carpentry Max Fendl
D-83627 Warngau/Wall

Carpentry and wooden
frame construction Heyd
D-74076 Heilbronn
www.zimmerei-heyd.de

Meschter Metalltechnik
D-49326 Melle
www.meschter.de

Zoth GmbH & Co. KG
D-56479 Westernohe
www.zoth.de

PARTNERS FROM ABROAD

Denaldi Legnami sas
I-15033 Casale Monferrato AL
www.denaldi.it

Holzplus
A-5585 Unternberg, Austria
www.holzplus.com

ASSEMBLY SUPPORT

Markus Bensch
René Eich
Lino Gozzi
Manuel Hermann
Manuel Hertlein
Ute und Simon McGuire

Joseph Oberauer
Axel Stache
Daniel Henzold
Peter Hoock
Florian Heugel
Cem Yapici

COLLABORATOR

Cristina Caldieri
Andrea Cigolini
Claudia Horn
Clara Reichertz

Jan Fuchs
Peter Lalowski
Louis Beck

VISUALISATION

Cristina Caldieri / Andrea Cigolini (Cone-Treehouse,
Winding Snake, Palm Fiction, Jungle House,
Water Lily, Beneath the leaves, Coldwater, Treehouse
Lodge Schrems, Hotel Extension in Mendoza,
On the Roof, The Kitchen)
Claudia Horn (Lightning, Bâlvedere Treehouse)
Jan Martin Fuchs (Black Crystal, Dark
Room, Lug ins Land, Trifels, K1, Loop)

TRAINEES 2004–2021

Benjamin Cury
Bettina Biernoth
Sávio Fernandes
Sandra Fröhlich
Michael Hormann
Henrik Isermann
Björn Krüger
Esther-Marie Kröger
Diana Levin
Benjamin Matzke
Dennis Ötting
Jan Martin Reiss
Miriam Reuter
Martin Schlesier

Marisa Diyana Shahrir
Cindy Rademake
Tania Pimentel
Sören Niederschmidt
Leonard Germann
Leo Althoff
Fabian Homburg
Sabrina Severin
Benjamin Behrens
Lukas Wagner
Jonathan Förster
Steffen Topitsch
Erik Völkel

PHOTOGRAPHERS

ALASDAIR JARDINE

Treehouse Plendelhof
Treehouse Wencke
Treehouse Lake Tegern
Pear Treehouse
Lookout Station
Treehouse Eilenriede
Between Alder and Oak
Scout Treehouse Almke (photos outside)
Between Magnolia and Pine
World of Living
Treehouse Bachstelze
Treehouse Djuren
Frog Prince
Bâlvedere Treehouse
'Baumgeflüster' Treehouse Hotel

www.jardinemedia.de

ANDREAS WENNING

Casa Girafa
Treehouse Louisa
Treehouse Apulia
Caporea Birch Pavilion
Caporea Birch Pavilion in Turin
Winding Nest
Oldenburg Castle Garden
Gibbon experience in Bokeo
Child's treehouse in Frankfurt/Main
Ivenacker oaks, old lime
Landscape photos for the projects
Water Lily and Beneath the Leaves
Luis and Jorins Hideaway
Construction site photos

ANDRÉ DOGBEY

Observation Tower at the Marshy
Woodland in Bollenhagen
Treehouse – Hotel Elbinselhof Krautsand
Lütetsburg Treehouse – Lodges
Dark Room

MARKUS BOLLEN

Copper Cube, Solling Treehouse
Treehouse On the Spree
The Treehouse
Around the Oak

www.markusbollen.de

FURTHER PHOTOGRAPHERS

Walter Keber: West runway protests
Tim Wagner: Hambach Forest pictures
Martin Zeller: Tree Assessment pictures
Harald Melcher: Korowai in Irian Jaya
Nico Marziali: Meditation Treehouse
Tim Mrzyglod: Scout Treehouse Almke (photos inside)
Dirk Vogel: Nut Room
Michael Döring: Cliff Treehouse
Aram Radomski: Project LOOP
Laura Fiorio: Urban Treehouse
Sven Adelaide: Oldenburg Castle Garden
Josef Herfert: Treehouse Lodge Schrems
Michael Dieck: Treehouse 'Wache 6'
Gerardo Gaetani d'Aragona: Casa Emilio
Ferdinand Graf Luckner: Oval Office, Green Dwelling
Michael O'Neal: Black Crystal

AUTHOR

CO-AUTHORS

Prof. Dr. Eberhard Syring

Born in 1951. He completed a carpentry apprenticeship, studied architecture in Bremen, and then began his professional career. Since 1990 his work has focused on the history of architecture. He obtained his doctorate by the University of Bremen in 1999 for his work on changing interpretations of architecture in the 20th century. Since 2004 he is professor of Architectural Theory and Architectural History at the School of Architecture in Bremen and academic director of the Centre for Building Culture.

Dipl.-Ing. Klaus Schöpe

Born in 1956. He studied Landscape Planning at the Technical University of Berlin, and has worked in gardening, landscaping, and tree husbandry. Founded *Baumbüro* in 1998. He is an officially appointed and sworn expert for tree statics, tree husbandry, and tree surveying since 1999.

Dipl. Ind. Des. Martin Zeller

Born in Munich in 1963. He studied Industrial Design and Architecture at the Munich University of Applied Sciences, then worked in planning offices in Munich, Nuremberg and Stuttgart. In 2006 training as Tree Engineer at the Karlsruhe Institute of Technology. Founded the expert office Baumzentrum Kaiserstuhl in 2007. Since 2020 he is lecturer for tree engineering at TU Dortmund.

Andreas Wenning with his sons Luis and Jorin in their treehouse

DIPL.-ING. ARCHITECT, ANDREAS WENNING

Born in 1965. Trained as carpenter in Weinheim in South Germany, he studied architecture in Bremen and worked for firms in Germany and Australia. Founded the architecture firm *Baumraum* in 2003 with projects in various countries in Europe, Argentina, Brazil Russia, China and the United States. Lectures and teaching work, numerous publications in Germany and abroad.

www.baumraum.de

The *Deutsche Nationalbibliothek* lists this publication in
the *Deutsche Nationalbibliografie*; detailed bibliographic data
are available in the Internet at http://dnb.d-nb.de.

ISBN 978-3-86922-736-8

TRANSLATION

Eva-Raphaela Jaksch
Clarice Knowles
Vicki May
Greg Lawson
Simon Doyle

EDITING

Katja Zeilhofer
Damian Leaf

DESIGN

André Dogbey
Cristina Montellano López

COVER DESIGN

Cristina Montellano López (4th edition)

PRINTING

Tiger Printing (Hong Kong) Co., Ltd.
www.tigerprinting.hk

This publication is also available in German (ISBN 978-3-86922-189-2)